Inheritance
and the Inequality
of Material Wealth

Studies in Social Economics

TITLES PUBLISHED

STUDIES IN SOCIAL ECONOMICS

John A. Brittain

Inheritance and the Inequality of Material Wealth

THE BROOKINGS INSTITUTION
Washington, D.C.

Library of Congress Cataloging in Publication Data:

Brittain, John A
  Inheritance and the inequality of material wealth.

  (Studies in social economics)
  Includes bibliographical references and index.
  1. Inheritance and succession—United States.
2. Wealth—United States.   I. Title.   II. Series.
HB715.B739   330.1'6   77-91814
ISBN 0-8157-1084-4
ISBN 0-8157-1083-6 pbk.

9 8 7 6 5 4 3 2 1

THE BROOKINGS INSTITUTION is an independent organization devoted to nonpartisan research, education, and publication in economics, government, foreign policy, and the social sciences generally. Its principal purposes are to aid in the development of sound public policies and to promote public understanding of issues of national importance.

The Institution was founded on December 8, 1927, to merge the activities of the Institute for Government Research, founded in 1916, the Institute of Economics, founded in 1922, and the Robert Brookings Graduate School of Economics and Government, founded in 1924.

The Board of Trustees is responsible for the general administration of the Institution, while the immediate direction of the policies, program, and staff is vested in the President, assisted by an advisory committee of the officers and staff. The by-laws of the Institution state: "It is the function of the Trustees to make possible the conduct of scientific research, and publication, under the most favorable conditions, and to safeguard the independence of the research staff in the pursuit of their studies and in the publication of the results of such studies. It is not a part of their function to determine, control, or influence the conduct of particular investigations or the conclusions reached."

The President bears final responsibility for the decision to publish a manuscript as a Brookings book. In reaching his judgment on the competence, accuracy, and objectivity of each study, the President is advised by the director of the appropriate research program and weighs the views of a panel of expert outside readers who report to him in confidence on the quality of the work. Publication of a work signifies that it is deemed a competent treatment worthy of public consideration but does not imply endorsement of conclusions or recommendations.

The Institution maintains its position of neutrality on issues of public policy in order to safeguard the intellectual freedom of the staff. Hence interpretations or conclusions in Brookings publications should be understood to be solely those of the authors and should not be attributed to the Institution, to its trustees, officers, or other staff members, or to the organizations that support its research.

Foreword

Economists and other social scientists have devoted less attention to inequality in the distribution of wealth than to inequality in the distribution of income. The relative neglect is puzzling, because inequality of wealth is far more pronounced and is known to be a major cause of inequality of income and other measures of economic success.

In this study John A. Brittain evaluates the role of material inheritance in the perpetuation of inequality of wealth. He believes that in a society that seeks to reward productivity it is important to isolate the effects of gifts and bequests—that is, wealth acquired without effort. After reviewing the earlier work of British and American scholars on the transfer of wealth from one generation to the next, Brittain presents new evidence derived from Internal Revenue Service estimates of the distribution of net worth by age, sex, and marital status. A portion of his analysis is built on the patterns of inheritance by men and women revealed by a sample of families in the Cleveland area in the mid-1960s.

Brittain finds that gifts and bequests, on the average, account for half or more of the net worth of very wealthy men and for most of the net worth of equally wealthy women. He weighs this finding against a recently suggested alternative explanation: that wealth increases with age, yielding a relatively benign form of inequality at any given time. His conclusion is that the age-related component is a minor reason for the persistence of wealth inequality, far subordinate to the intergenerational transfer of material wealth.

This volume is a companion to Brittain's *The Inheritance of Economic Status* (Brookings, 1977), which dealt with the effects of socioeconomic background on the educational attainment, occupational status, income, and quality of residence of sons and daughters. The earlier work also considered the role of education and marital selection in the determination of the ultimate economic status of sons and daughters. The present study concentrates instead on the effects of material inheritance on the distribution of material wealth, as distinct from income and other dimensions of human endowment or earning power considered in the companion volume.

Although the author relied primarily on public data sources, he is especially grateful to Marvin B. Sussman, Judith N. Cates, and David T. Smith, who made available the Cleveland data on inheritance patterns, and to the Russell Sage Foundation, which sponsored their original research. He also wishes to thank A. B. Atkinson, W. Irwin Gillespie, Gerald R. Jantscher, Guy H. Orcutt, Joseph A. Pechman, S. J. Prais, James D. Smith, and others who offered criticism and comments on the manuscript. He further acknowledges the valuable research assistance of K. Wendy Holt, Lawrence Moore, and Deborah Ramirez. The manuscript was checked for accuracy by Evelyn P. Fisher and Brookings staff members under her direction; it was edited by Tadd Fisher. The index was prepared by BevAnne Ross, and the figures were drawn by Clare and Frank Ford.

The author is a senior fellow in the Brookings Economic Studies program. His study was supported by a grant from the Ford Foundation and is the fifteenth in the Brookings series of Studies in Social Economics, a program of research on selected problems in the fields of health, education, social security, and welfare. The views expressed in the study are the author's and should not be ascribed to the Ford Foundation or to the officers, trustees, or other staff members of the Brookings Institution.

BRUCE K. MAC LAURY
President

December 1977
Washington, D.C.

Contents

chapter one Introduction

*The ownership of personal or material productive
capacity is based upon a complex mixture of
inheritance, luck, and effort, probably in that order
of relative importance.*
FRANK H. KNIGHT, *Quarterly Journal of Economics*, August 1923

The transfer of wealth from one generation to the next
is a neglected area of economic analysis. It has long been suspected that
intergenerational gifts and inheritances are a major factor in the perpetuation of economic inequality, but solid evidence is quite limited. The objectives here are to review the earlier work of British and American scholars on this question, add new evidence concerning the United States, and
indicate hopeful areas for future investigation.[1] The emphasis in this study
is on explicit material wealth transfers—inheritances, interpreted as including gifts as well as bequests. This focus is adopted despite recognition
that intergenerational transfers of "human wealth," or earning power, may
play an even larger role in maintaining the overall inequality of economic
status.[2] A stress on material transfers seems entirely appropriate in any
analysis of the extremes of the wealth and income distributions. Gifts and
bequests to young lawyers may not have much to do with the contrasts be-

I am indebted to Walter S. Salant for calling my attention to Frank H. Knight's
conjecture about the important influence of inheritance, which anticipated a major
conclusion documented in this monograph.
1. The pros and cons of reducing wealth inequality will not be considered here,
except with respect to a suggested contrast between inherited and other types of
wealth. For a more general discussion of the extensive literature on incentives, the
desirability of a leisure class, and so on, see Alan A. Tait, *The Taxation of Personal
Wealth* (University of Illinois Press, 1967).
2. Transfers of human wealth, or capital, include not only the provision of educational opportunity to one's children but also the conscious or even willy-nilly transmission of economic status to children via genetic influences or an advantageous
family environment. I have considered the latter in John A. Brittain, *The Inheritance
of Economic Status* (Brookings Institution, 1977).

tween their economic status and that of young laborers, but such transfers clearly generated most of the wealth differential between the Rockefeller brothers and most other sets of brothers.

In any analysis of economic inequality among individuals it is tempting to try to separate the inherited and contemporary factors most likely to perpetuate it. In the case of wealth inequality the contrast is between wealth accumulation via intergenerational transfers and independent accumulation.[3] Although these types of accumulation cannot be separated into two watertight compartments, the distinction is important for ethical and policy reasons.

A traditional view holds that the inheritance of material advantage stands in sharp contrast to the accumulation of wealth through a person's own efforts during his lifetime. An inheritance entails no productive activity. Accumulation resulting from one's own efforts usually entails some such activity, although it may be facilitated by family background and may not be universally admired. This broad distinction is important for purposes of wealth taxation policy. Polar examples, from a tax standpoint, of the two forms of wealth accumulation are (1) inherited material wealth, and (2) a lifetime accumulation of savings out of earnings that vary only with age. (If saving ratios also varied only with age, the second form of wealth accumulation would yield a relatively benign form of wealth inequality among persons of different ages.) The first form has long been a widely accepted target for taxation, the second less so. Although other types of current accumulation, such as capital gains, are appropriately subjected to tax, it is the direct inheritance of material wealth, openly and explicitly creating inequality of "life chances," that has been seen as the most defensible basis for wealth taxation.[4]

Even though the importance of inheritance in generating fortunes has not been widely debated, there is a wide spectrum of opinion. In a classic study published in 1929 Wedgwood claimed a major role for intergenerational transfers.

The evidence . . . supports the opinion that, in the great majority of the cases, the large fortunes of one generation belong to the children of those who pos-

3. "Independent accumulation" is intended to refer to all types of accumulation not representing direct intergenerational transfers. Some forms of independent accumulation, of course, can be facilitated by other types of parental influence.

4. At least that has been a commonly held view of economists over the years. Whether it is shared by the general population is debatable. A cry of outrage greeted presidential candidate George McGovern's call in 1972 for a very heavy inheritance tax. It is also worth noting that Congress voted in 1977 to substantially increase the estate tax exemption. The only reductions in the nominally high estate tax rates were very modest, however, and at the highest wealth levels only.

sessed the large fortunes of the preceding generation. Even after the windfalls of the war inflation period, the rich men who have sprung from parents with insignificant resources are almost certainly a minority of their class. The attention which that minority attracts seems to be due to the fact that those who compose it are exceptional phenomena rather than numerous.[5]

On the other hand, the consensus of articles appearing in *Fortune* in the last twenty years (and discussed below) is that about one-half of the very wealthy have been self-made men. Although these conclusions pertain to different times and places, they illustrate the breadth of opinion.[6] These differences cannot be confidently resolved here, but it may be useful to offer another evaluation of the evidence.

The Observed Inequality of Material Wealth and Its Significance

Few are likely to challenge the casual observation that the inequality of material wealth is very pronounced. Before considering the importance of inheritance as a perpetuator of this form of inequality, however, it is appropriate to review briefly the evidence on wealth inequality. Since this is a complex subject, the results naturally vary with alternative definitions of wealth, the recipient unit, and measures of inequality. For example, the exclusion of substantial wealth held in trust will be mentioned as a shortcoming of the available evidence, but it should also be recognized that such wealth is a less liquid asset than an unrestricted claim. The primary interest here is in the relative shares of total net worth held by top individual wealthholders. Trust holdings, accrued pension claims, and wealth-splitting will be mentioned only as qualifications of the official evidence.

Estimating the distribution of the individual wealth of the living on the basis of the reported wealth of the dead by the "estate multiplier" technique is generally thought to offer the most accurate picture.[7] The major

5. Josiah Wedgwood, *The Economics of Inheritance* (London: Routledge, 1929; Kennekat, 1971). The quotation is from p. 164 of the 1929 edition.

6. The importance of inheritance is discounted even more in Herman P. Miller, *Rich Man, Poor Man* (Crowell, 1971 ed.), pp. 156–58, and in Stanley Lebergott, *The American Economy: Income, Wealth, and Want* (Princeton University Press, 1976), especially pp. 149–78.

7. The only official estimates of the distribution of wealth are those of the Internal Revenue Service, and they are derived by this method, which entails applying mortality rates to the distribution of decedents' estates. The other two approaches are the capitalization of property income—usually that reported on tax returns—and the sample survey. The former must rely on aggregate rates of return, and the latter is subject to the typical shortfall found in survey reports. Some of the results from the principal wealth survey in this country are summarized later.

study by Lampman covered data for the wealthiest 1.6 percent of all decedents in 1953, the year studied in most detail. On the basis of these data Lampman offered estimates of the share of the top 1 percent of living individual wealthholders in the national wealth. The largest swings in this share that he found between selected years in the 34-year interval studied were from 32 percent in 1922 up to 38 percent in 1929, down to 22 percent in 1949, and up to 28 percent in 1956.[8] Despite some apparent cyclical swings, these data generally support the view that the shape of the upper tail of the wealth distribution has been rather stable over the long run; at most, the estimates for the eight years studied suggest a slight downward trend.

More recent estimates of the share of the top 1 percent of all persons in total net worth have been presented by Smith and Franklin and show an even more remarkable stability: 27 percent in 1958 and 1962, 26 percent in 1969, and 27 percent in 1972.[9] Taken together, these estimates plus Lampman's suggest that the very high nominal estate tax rates established in the thirties have done little to reduce the inequality of wealth—even over a substantial period of time. If the estate tax had been a potent force, the great increase in rates would have produced a clear downward trend —certainly one discernible by the seventies.

Even the high degree of inequality indicated by these estimates is probably substantially understated in several ways. Perhaps the major omission is that of most personal wealth held in trusts—the great bulk of which escapes inclusion in estate tax returns. For example, Smith and Franklin estimated that among the top 0.5 percent of all wealthholders in 1969, assets in trust amounted to only 9 percent of the wealth.[10] Jantscher, however, has argued that due to the exclusion of most wealth in trust from estate tax returns, almost certainly the true trust holdings of these persons were much larger than the Smith-Franklin figures indicate.[11]

8. Robert J. Lampman, *The Share of Top Wealth-Holders in National Wealth, 1922–56* (Princeton University Press for the National Bureau of Economic Research, 1962). See especially p. 228 and chart 36, p. 224.

9. James D. Smith and Stephen D. Franklin, estimates reported in U.S. Bureau of the Census, *Statistical Abstract of the United States, 1975* (Government Printing Office, 1975), p. 410. For a recent analysis of wealth distribution in Britain, see A. B. Atkinson and A. J. Harrison, *The Distribution of Personal Wealth in Britain* (Cambridge University Press, forthcoming).

10. James D. Smith and Stephen D. Franklin, "The Concentration of Personal Wealth, 1922–1969," *American Economic Review*, vol. 64 (May 1974, *Papers and Proceedings, 1973*), p. 166.

11. Gerald R. Jantscher and George Cooper, manuscript in preparation on estate and gift taxation.

Most of the wealth in trust form is concentrated in the very high wealth brackets, and its exclusion clearly understates the inequality of wealth, even though it must be recognized that wealth held in trust is relatively illiquid. One clue to the magnitude of this omission is to be found in the comparison in table 1-1 of the size distribution of the bank-administered personal trusts and estates with the distribution of the wealth of individuals. The table shows that bank-administered trusts and estates are relatively more common in the highest wealth ranks. Even though the data cover only 49 banks, there are more than one-quarter as many trusts and estates in the top wealth class as there are individual wealthholders. In the lowest class there are only about 6 for every 100 wealthholders. Although there is no way to separate trusts and estates in these figures, it seems apparent that the concentration of trusts is greater than the concentration of individual wealth. Since most wealth in trusts is excluded from the estate tax statistics, the downward bias in the official estate multiplier estimates is probably greater the higher the wealth rank.[12]

While the observed share of the top wealth classes may be understated in the ways described above, Feldstein has recently emphasized a bias working in the opposite direction.[13] He imputes the present value of an-

12. Other important limitations of the estate multiplier method, in addition to the meagerness of the data base, are problems associated with the data and the method itself. Rough estimates by Harriss suggest that estate evaluations may average 10 percent below "objective" estimates, which themselves contain a substantial arbitrary component. (C. Lowell Harriss, "Wealth Estimates as Affected by Audit of Estate Tax Returns," *National Tax Journal*, vol. 2 [December 1949], pp. 316–33.) The estimates could be improved if the Internal Revenue Service used audited returns in its estimates. The method has traditionally assumed that the dead are a representative sample of the living of the same age and sex and that available age-sex mortality rates can be used to derive estimates of the wealth of the living. Lampman could make only a rough allowance for the fact that the mortality rates of the wealthy are probably relatively low; if the extra longevity of the wealthy is inadequately measured, the blown-up frequencies for the living top wealthholders are biased downward. Generally this can be expected to bias downward the estimated relative share of the top wealth ranks, but there may be exceptions. (For the effects of alternative mortality rates on estimated wealth inequality, see A. B. Atkinson and A. J. Harrison, "Mortality Multipliers and the Estate Duty Method," *Oxford Bulletin of Economics and Statistics*, vol. 37 [February 1975], pp. 13–28.) In any case it seems likely that broadened availability of medical care may have reduced mortality rate differentials in recent years. Another problem is the tendency for the wealth of a decedent to have been partially depleted by wealth-splitting via gifts, trusts, and so forth. Although a wealthy man's gift of one-half his wealth to his five children reduces measured inequality among individuals, the practical effect among broad wealth ranks may be minimal; for example, it might reduce the share of the top 1 percent but correspondingly increase the share of the next 4 percent.

13. See Martin Feldstein, "Social Security and the Distribution of Wealth," *Journal of the American Statistical Association*, vol. 71 (December 1976), pp. 800–807,

Table 1-1. Comparison of the Net Worth of Bank-Administered Personal Trusts and Estates with That of Individual Wealthholders, 1969

Net worth (thousands of dollars)	Number of bank-administered personal trusts and estates	Number of individual wealthholders
300–500	24,000ᵃ	414,000ᵃ
500–1,000	19,398	228,000ᵃ
1,000–5,000	12,409	111,322
5,000 and over	2,412	9,330

Sources: Data on trusts and estates administered by 49 banks are from U.S. Securities and Exchange Commission, *Report on Institutional Investment Study*, vol. 2 (March 10, 1971), p. 431. Data on individual wealth is from U.S. Internal Revenue Service, *Statistics of Income—1969, Personal Wealth Estimated from Estate Tax Returns* (Government Printing Office, 1969), p. 19.
a. Estimated roughly by algebraic linear interpolation after double logarithmic Pareto-type transformations. (See table 2-2, note a.) Since the 24,000 figure depended on a point in the nonlinear range, nonlinear graphical interpolation was used to derive the estimate in this particular case.

ticipated social security pensions to total wealth classes.[14] Since pension claims are much more equally distributed than material wealth, this imputation reduces the relative share of the top wealth ranks. For example, one estimate by Feldstein shows the share in the national wealth of the top 1 percent falling from 28 percent to 19 percent in 1962 when his estimates of "social security wealth" are included. If this imputation is accepted, it seems likely that the effect would be to offset the previously discussed downward biases. Even so the rough indication is that the top 1 percent probably own about one-quarter of all wealth.

In some ways the inequality revealed in across-the-board wealth distribution is more striking than the large share of the top 1 percent. The main evidence on this is that of Projector and Weiss for 1962.[15] Their survey showed the top 6 percent of families owning 57 percent of all wealth and the top 16 percent owning 75 percent of it. The shares of the low ranks are even more revealing. The net worth of 11 percent of all

especially p. 804. For earlier work in the British context, see A. B. Atkinson, "The Distribution of Wealth and the Individual Life-Cycle," *Oxford Economic Papers*, n.s., vol. 23 (July 1971), pp. 239–54.
14. Feldstein does not impute the present value of future earnings; presumably he is willing to maintain the distinction between material and human wealth. It is implied that estimated accrued pension claims are a part of material wealth. This seems appropriate, since the pension claims are a form of saving generally derived from pension contributions representing income forgone.
15. Dorothy S. Projector and Gertrude S. Weiss, *Survey of Financial Characteristics of Consumers* (Board of Governors of the Federal Reserve System, 1966), especially pp. 96 and 136.

families was negative, 5 percent were listed at zero, and 12 percent at under $1,000—a total of 28 percent of households with wealth less than $1,000. Perhaps most impressive of all is that 46 percent of all families had wealth under $5,000; these families (most of the bottom half) are credited with owning only 2 percent of all wealth.[16]

This capsule picture of the inequality of wealth seems clear enough, despite some underlying weaknesses in the data. But it presents a form of inequality that is of course far greater than the inequality of income, which includes returns from human capital as well as material wealth.[17] It is sometimes suggested that material wealth is not relevant and that it is only the inequality of income that matters. Why then do economists remain concerned with the inequality of material wealth?

It may be appropriate to mention first a concern with the distribution of wealth that has recently been gaining prominence. Legislators and others are asking whether the emphasis on the inequality of income may be excluding an important issue in the problem of economic inequality. Obviously wealth is an important determinant of economic security over and above that provided by income. Who is better off with his $10,000 income—a $10,000-a-year wage earner or a coupon clipper who owns $150,000 worth of bonds? There is no pat answer. The wage earner can hope for rising real earnings, while the wealthholder may be forced to choose between declining real income and more risky investments. But the holder of material wealth has far greater immediate security than the holder of human capital with equal income.

Weisbrod and Hansen have stressed that wealth in the form of liquid capital has an importance over and above the income it generates.[18] They built on the acceptable proposition that given two persons of equal income, the one with the greater wealth is better off because of the added

16. This 2 percent figure is the sum for individuals with positive net worth; it has not been reduced by the negative net worth of those at the bottom of the wealth pyramid, although that would seem appropriate.

17. The inequality of the distribution of human *plus* material wealth is probably roughly the same as the inequality of income, especially if income includes imputed returns to capital, such as undistributed profits. This variant of income sums up the returns to both human and material wealth. If human wealth were imputed to individuals on the basis of their earnings, the wealth distribution would be more equal. If income were then roughly proportional to wealth by wealth rank, inequality in the two distributions would be about the same.

18. Burton A. Weisbrod and W. Lee Hansen, "An Income–Net Worth Approach to Measuring Economic Welfare," *American Economic Review,* vol. 58 (December 1968), pp. 1315–29.

security he possesses. They devised a measurement of welfare combining
the lifetime annuity that could be purchased with the wealth, and income
proper. The need to consider both dimensions is especially apparent in
the contrasting positions of the young and the old. Young people usually
have higher incomes relative to their net worth. On the other hand, the
wealth held by older people may well compensate for relatively low money
incomes—especially if capital gains are accruing. In such circumstances
money income is a deceptively low indicator of a person's purchasing
power.[19] Material wealth has another important feature: in addition to
providing security it is the source of what has been traditionally regarded
as "unearned" income. Even when a person invests savings from his earnings, the return is classified as unearned since no further effort must be
expended to obtain it. It has been a tradition to regard unearned income
and the capital generating it as especially appropriate targets of taxation.
A better understanding of the determinants of material wealth would be
relevant to such tax policy. And, finally, still another feature of material
wealth is that its extreme concentration may confer power on a few that
is hazardous to democratic institutions.[20]

Some of the reasons for the special interest in the distribution of wealth
have been usefully summarized as follows:

Attitudes toward the inequality of wealth depend on views of its causes. Suppose it could be shown that wealth was unequally distributed mainly because
income was unequally distributed and hence some people saved more, in

19. The annuity approach of Weisbrod and Hansen is a step forward in dealing
with this problem. Consider, however, the case of A and B who have equal income
and wealth of $10,000 each but are 30 and 80 years old, respectively. The annuity
criterion has the older man far better off because he can convert his wealth into a
greater lifetime annual consuming power. But his life expectancy is far less; moreover, the bequest motive is very strong for many wealthholders. The younger man, A,
can expect his nest egg to grow steadily, increasing his own security and potential
consumption and enabling him to do very well by his heirs or charity. The Weisbrod-
Hansen approach has also been criticized more formally in an interesting piece by
A. B. Atkinson, "Measuring Economic Welfare—A Comment" (London: City University, 1970; processed).

20. Material wealth is not, of course, the only source of political power. Within
the apparatus of the state, for example, men of modest means have held enormous
power. The point here is that the concentration of wealth facilitates the concentration
of power—sometimes including that exercised by those who are not wealthy. So even
though material wealth may not be the dominant factor in overall economic inequality, its determinants are of special significance. Moreover, the strength of the case for
taxing it depends on the extent to which individuals obtain it without independent
effort. Thus the appropriate policy toward wealth inequality depends on the process
of its generation—especially the extent to which it is inherited.

consequence accumulating more wealth. Then wealth inequality would not be a separate social problem but only another facet of income inequality. Though it might be expedient to attempt to reduce inequality by redistributing wealth, a more fundamental policy would be to attack the problem at its source and seek for ways to equalize income opportunities. If, on the other hand, it turns out that the primary cause of wealth inequality is inheritance, then, if one is serious about reducing inequality, one would presumably seek for ways to redistribute wealth directly.[21]

Competing Explanations of the Inequality of Wealth

In this study the factors underlying wealth inequality are placed in two primary, not perfectly separable, categories: (1) inheritance (intergenerational), including both gifts and bequests and the going rate of return on them;[22] and (2) independent accumulation of two types—saving out of earnings and the going return on it, and extraordinary returns on investment.[23]

An intergenerational transfer is due to forces over which the recipient has little control and is rarely a reward for productive effort. Independent accumulation, though it does not necessarily derive from any universally admired contribution to society, depends at least in part on some activity of the wealthholder himself. The assumption is that the former is the more appropriate target of public intervention to alleviate the inequality it engenders. This two-way breakdown of types of wealth accumulation is very broad and is not put forward as a pure distinction between unearned and earned accumulation. In the case of transfers, for example, a bequest by a father may have been strenuously earned by him, but it was not earned by his heir. On the other hand, independent first-generation accumulation

21. Nicholas Oulton, "Inheritance and the Distribution of Wealth," *Oxford Economic Papers,* n.s., vol. 28 (March 1976), p. 86.

22. Intragenerational transfers are not considered of fundamental importance here. Thus, for example, a bequest by a decedent male to his widow is not viewed as affecting the distribution of wealth. This approach is not entirely satisfactory, since one person is better off with a given amount of wealth than were the original two persons. The data offer no way to allow for varying family size, however.

23. It should be repeated that the phrase "independent accumulation" does not necessarily indicate the fruits of productive or socially desirable activity—simply that it is not traceable to past generations. Extraordinary returns, for example, might include those deriving from what has been called the "internalization" of the benefits of public programs, as when wealthy farmers gain disproportionate benefits from subsidy programs (see Howard P. Tuckman, *The Economics of the Rich* [Random House, 1973], p. 8).

—even out of wages or salaries—is often aided by a favorable start in life or even by sheer luck.[24] The view here is simply that the distinction between transfers and other forms of accumulation is useful and relevant to social policy.

The dichotomy adopted here submerges various other issues of interest and importance. For example, no distinction is made between inheritance from one's own parents and other types of inheritance—such as inheritance derived (presumably indirectly) from parents-in-law. It seems highly likely that men tend to marry women with a wealth background similar to their own. This type of marital selection—"assortative mating" —has been clearly observed for measures of socioeconomic background other than material wealth alone.[25] A similar association of the parental wealth of husbands and wives seems highly likely. From the present point of view, marital selection may increase or decrease one's chance of a sizable inheritance. A surviving spouse can hope to inherit wealth from a decedent spouse that was actually transferred from the latter's parents. There is no doubt that this process helps perpetuate the concentration of wealth, but its relevance to the evaluation of inheritance is somewhat ambiguous. A study of the role of inheritance in generating the wealth of *families* would appropriately include the inheritances of both spouses; in the case of widows or widowers, it would include that portion of inheritance from a decedent that could be attributed to his or her inheritance from parents.

Since the available data on wealth pertain primarily to individuals, it seems best to confine a study of the effect of inheritance to inheritance by an individual from his parents. This is essentially the coverage of the analysis of inheritance by married men and women to be presented later. There is no intention here, however, to dismiss the importance of explicit transfers traceable to in-laws or of the unmeasurable advantages of having wealthy in-laws.

The classification of wealth into inherited and noninherited components was motivated by their contrasting policy implications and is not intended to downplay the enormous variation within the category of in-

---

24. Although earnings offer incentives for productive activity, it is not being suggested here that earnings are *always* a less appropriate target for taxation than inheritances. For example, there is little reason to believe that a sudden increase in a rock music star's salary from $100 to $10,000 a week is necessarily either a needed incentive or a good indication of a 100-fold gain in productivity. It is only suggested that earnings, unlike inheritances, are usually associated with productive activity and that this is relevant to tax policy.

25. For example, see Brittain, *The Inheritance of Economic Status*, chap. 4.

dependent accumulation. Atkinson has appraised the latter as a rival to inheritance in the amassing of large fortunes.[26] Nonetheless, his key point was that the great "new" fortunes grew out of truly extraordinary returns captured in a small minority of capitalist ventures rather than from gradual saving and the gathering of interest. Indeed he stressed that the really large fortunes could not possibly be accumulated by an average earner in this way.

Atkinson's thesis has been elaborated in an important essay by Thurow, who varies the theme slightly by noting that "large fortunes are passed from generation to generation and great fortunes occur suddenly."[27] His point is that even the current inherited Rockefeller, Mellon, Ford, and Du Pont fortunes were very quickly accumulated in the past. Like Atkinson, he notes that most wealth does not come from a patient process of saving and reinvestment. The great fortunes are accumulated too quickly for that to be the source.

The way Atkinson and Thurow view the process of accumulating wealth—especially the achievement of great wealth—may be contrasted with the picture drawn by neoclassical economics. In that world each person starts with two main endowments—inheritance and earning power. Subject to various constraints, a person will tend to increase his wealth by saving and reinvestment. Inequalities generally increase over time because the wealthier are apt to save more. But fortune-building is limited by the heavy constraints on saving and an assumed tendency to consume capital upon retirement. In other words, the neoclassical picture is one of gradual accumulation followed by decumulation; this is traditionally known as the life-cycle hypothesis.

Some empirical criticism of the life-cycle hypothesis and its relevance to evaluating the importance of inheritance will be considered in detail later, but some of Atkinson's and Thurow's generalizations should be noted here. An inherent tendency for wealth to increase is plausible, although fortunes do not (and cannot) grow out of routine saving, nor are they generally dissipated upon retirement. Wealthy people continue accumulating in their old age, despite tax incentives to make inter vivos gifts to their children. Thurow attributes this to a motive left out of the neoclassical construct—the desire for economic power. In his view this mo-

26. A. B. Atkinson, *Unequal Shares: Wealth in Britain* (London: Penguin, 1972), chap. 3.

27. Lester C. Thurow, *Generating Inequality: Mechanisms of Distribution in the U.S. Economy* (Basic Books, 1975), p. 129.

tive is excluded by the assumption of perfect competition. This could be illustrated by a current controversy: a natural gas producer could not attain price objectives through exercising economic power—for example, by withholding investment; someone else would move in and pursue a "normal profit." Such competition, however, is often limited in the real world; "the holder of wealth has some leverage to redesign his family, private charities, the economy, and the political structure in his own image."[28] For Thurow this is a key explanation for the failure of the aged to decumulate (as they are predicted to do under the life-cycle hypothesis). Their failure to draw down their wealth helps perpetuate inequality.

How are great fortunes amassed in the first place? Thurow turns to disequilibrium in real capital markets for his explanation. He notes the extreme variance of rates of return across industries and firms and adds that in a dynamic economy new opportunities offering high rates of return appear occasionally, as in the two great fortunes made in McDonald's hamburgers and Hartz Mountain pet food and accessories. Investors in the financial markets bid up the share values of such high-yielding real investments—and often to very high "multiples," or price-earning ratios. "Large instantaneous fortunes are created when the financial markets capitalize new above-average rate of return investments to yield average rate of return financial investments."[29]

Finally, for Thurow the "random walk" literature on security prices offers an explanation of the pronounced skewness of the distribution of wealth. Since all information is quickly capitalized into the price of an asset, it is of no value, and investing at random becomes a rational approach. At least that may be what is happening, even if investors do not realize it. In effect the outcome of individual investments is randomized. Some investors pick firms that go out of business, others obtain average yields, and a tiny minority initiate or buy Xerox and become extremely wealthy. So in Thurow's view the random walk "will generate a highly skewed distribution of wealth regardless of the normal distribution of personal abilities and regardless of whether the economy does or does not start from an initial state of equality." He sums up his explanation of wealth inequality derived from the random walk hypothesis—a highly skewed distribution of wealth generated from a normal distribution of abilities:

Within risk and entrepreneurial ability classes, a random lottery is con-

28. Ibid., p. 142.
29. Ibid., p. 149.

ducted. As with all lotteries someone wins even though the probability of winning is very small. Chances of winning the lottery twice are almost non-existent, but once a great fortune is made it earns the market rate of return. . . . There is no feedback principle in the random walk that tends to equalize the distribution of wealth once it has become unequal.[30]

This theory of the cause of wealth inequality has been set forth here in some detail to contrast it with the life-cycle hypothesis and to balance the emphasis on inheritance in the present study. The discussion to follow emphasizes the distinction between inheritance and independent accumulation, although as noted previously, there can be no watertight distinction. Most great inherited fortunes were themselves independently accumulated at some prior stage. Despite this apparent conceptual ambiguity, it does seem both reasonable and useful to classify wealth in the hands of, say, the Rockefeller brothers as inherited—even if their grandfather accumulated the original fortune independently.

Interpretating wealth inequality as being due primarily to the highly skewed distribution of the outcomes of random lotteries has another important implication. Insofar as the degree of inequality is far greater than that attributable to differentials in ability and productivity, the case for public policy intervention and redistribution is comparable to that for inherited wealth. The less the rewards of wealth are associated with one's own contribution, the better the case for taxing them. So it should be conceded that much independent accumulation—like inheritance—may be almost in the nature of a windfall (and an especially appropriate target for taxation).[31] Even so, it is time to return to the present effort to isolate the role of inheritance in the generation of the wealth distribution prevailing at a given time. Inheritance remains one of the purest forms of "getting something for nothing."[32]

Preliminary Empirical Indications

Three broad areas of empirical research will be considered later. First, it may be useful to refer to some briefer ad hoc evaluations of the role of

30. Ibid., pp. 151, 153–54.

31. It is possible, of course, that people may be so enthusiastic about their own (or others') chances of receiving windfalls, such as lottery payoffs, that they may wish to leave the outcomes undisturbed by public policy. This would be consistent with the previously mentioned opposition to Senator McGovern's inheritance tax proposals in 1972.

32. It is not an entirely pure form, of course. An older person may (one way or another) extract a certain form of behavior from the heirs as a sine qua non of the inheritance—an informal quid pro quo.

inheritance in the generation of wealth. They illustrate well the methodo-logical difficulties encountered in such inquiries. The first studies to be discussed are all based on surveys.

Many lists of top wealthholders have been compiled in the past, but the *Fortune* studies by Smith and Louis reported in 1957, 1968, and 1973 offer the most current picture.[33] The 1957 report identified 155 indivi-duals estimated to hold $50 million or more, and the 1968 study found 153 over the $100 million mark. The studies assigned each individual to one of six wealth brackets.[34] It was conceded that perhaps as few as one-half of the actual number in these wealth classes had been tracked down. Even so, the indications of the part played by inheritance in the wealth of these individuals are useful.

The *Fortune* articles dealt explicitly but only in very broad terms with the role of inheritance and oil production in the building of fortunes. Smith indicated that 45 percent of the top 76 on the 1957 list "made their for-tunes on their own."[35] Similarly, Louis reports that about half of the top 66 wealth-owners in 1968 "inherited the bulk of it." A comparable result was presented for 1973 when 39 "new rich" were found to have acquired great wealth, starting from a small base. Louis also noted elsewhere that on the basis of the *Fortune* study in 1968 "both oil production and in-heritance have been declining as sources of great wealth."[36] The basis of this conclusion concerning inheritance is not at all clear, however; about half of the fortunes listed were designated as "inherited" in both 1957 and 1968.

The main problem with the *Fortune* analyses and with survey ap-proaches to the problem to date is that inheritance is generally treated as an either-or proposition. Apparently the bulk of the current value of holdings must have been inherited in order for the wealth to be classified as inherited. An advance beyond this qualitative approach might have

33. Richard Austin Smith, "The Fifty-Million-Dollar Man," *Fortune,* November 1957, pp. 176 ff.; Arthur M. Louis, "America's Centimillionaires," ibid., May 1968, pp. 152 ff.; and Arthur M. Louis, "The New Rich of the Seventies," ibid., September 1973, pp. 170 ff.

34. These figures include holdings of spouses, minor children, and trusts and foundations established by the listed wealthholder.

35. Smith, "Fifty-Million Dollar Man," p. 177. About 30 percent of these for-tunes were reported to be derived from oil, with nearly half of those also designated as "inherited."

36. Louis made this observation in a review of Ferdinand Lundberg, *The Rich and the Super-Rich: A Study in the Power of Money Today* (Lyle Stuart, 1968), in the Saturday Review, July 13, 1968, p. 30.

been achieved if a quantitative measure of the impact of inheritance had been developed and applied. Suppose, for illustrative purposes, that J. Paul Getty inherited $2 million from his parents; this might or might not have been a drop in the bucket in the building of his fortune.[37] It depends on what he had when he received it. If his net worth had been $2 million at the time of inheritance, it would certainly be reasonable to say that the inheritance proper constituted 50 percent of his wealth at that time. Would it also be reasonable to say that whether he had $1 billion or $2 billion when he died, 50 percent was due to inheritance? That is debatable, but a knowledge of the immediate impact of the inheritance on an heir's wealth is essential to evaluating its importance.[38]

Walter P. Inman, Jr., was credited with wealth of around $100 million in 1967 when he was an orphan 16 years of age. Louis has noted that "it would require a compound annual appreciation of only 6½ percent to make him a billionaire twice over by the time he is eligible for social security payment."[39] The original inheritance will not bulk large against his wealth in the distant future, but it would be difficult to say that the future fortune could be anything other than an inherited one, unless it could be shown that the rate of return he achieved was extraordinarily high. Even in the latter case, the opportunity to earn an unusually high rate of return might itself depend on the inherited family and business environment.

For any attempt to separate the roles of inheritance and independent accumulation in individual wealth-building, an analysis of the ratio of gifts and inheritance to total wealth immediately after the accession seems essential. As a first approximation in the simple case of a single inheritance, this ratio could generally be taken as the measure of its importance in today's fortune, whatever the subsequent yield achieved. This yield

37. Getty reported inheriting one-half million dollars from his father alone, but he also indicated that his father had provided the capital for his ventures over a considerable period of time in exchange for only 70 percent of the return. (See J. Paul Getty, *How to Be Rich* [Playboy Press, 1966], p. 5.) This might have been roughly equivalent to a total intergenerational transfer on the order of $2 million. In any case the hypothetical discussion in the text does not depend on the accuracy of this figure.

38. If the $2 million was already involved in a big winning venture and the inherited $2 million was simply put under the mattress, the latter would have had little to do with Getty's being a billionaire; but one would expect the new funds to be put to work even more aggressively than the old.

39. Louis, "America's Centimillionaires," p. 194. It should be added that much higher rates of return have been attained by mutual funds and market averages over a long period. See John A. Brittain, *The Payroll Tax for Social Security* (Brookings Institution, 1972), p. 196.

itself would also be germane to an explanation of the generation of wealth, but any return above the going rate might reasonably be attributed to independent accumulation. In any case the basic point here is that the ratio of the original value of inheritance to total current wealth is a gross understatement of the role of that inheritance.

It should also be noted that Louis stresses the changes between the 1957 and 1968 lists as one indication of the declining role of inheritance in wealth distribution. For example, 33 of his top 66 in 1968 were not on the list of the top 76 in 1957. This does not in any way suggest a declining importance of inheritance, however. Reranking is a continuing process in wealth and income distributions observed over time. Moreover, many who are new on the list are not necessarily nouveau riche; they may have had the way cleared for them by the deaths of others during the eleven-year interval. Those at the top rank have nowhere to go but down, and it would be necessary to show that *more* wealthy persons have dropped down *recently* than in the past in order to show a declining influence of inheritance.[40]

A second approach to the analysis of the role of material inheritance in the current wealth distribution is that offered by scientific sample surveys. Some detailed questions concerning the importance of gifts and inheritance were asked of the high-income group studied by Barlow, Brazer, and Morgan.[41] Respondents were asked what fraction of their total assets was accounted for by gifts and inheritance, respectively. Obviously a conscientious respondent would wonder how to evaluate an asset received years ago, and the interviewers were given a surprising instruction: the question was intended "to elicit the ratio of the *original* value of the gift or inheritance to the *current* value of total assets." Editors and coders were instructed "to make this definition prevail."[42] No explanation was given for this internally contradictory criterion. (Under it Getty's inheritance ratio would have been on the order of one-twentieth of 1 percent, as appraised in 1968.) Under this criterion (and some admittedly rough assumptions) the study found less than 20 percent of the personal wealth of this high-income group derived from gifts and inheritance. A low ratio

40. Put another way, a relatively low number of repeaters in the top ranks over time (among individuals and their heirs) would indeed indicate a relatively weak influence of inheritance; but Louis's finding of 33 repeaters out of 66 must be compared with the past or some other standard if it is to be persuasive evidence.

41. Robin Barlow, Harvey E. Brazer, and James N. Morgan, *Economic Behavior of the Affluent* (Brookings Institution, 1966), chap. 7.

42. Ibid., p. 89, note.

computed this way was to be expected, but in another estimate in which the authors allocated some appreciation to gifts and inheritance, they still attributed less than one-fifth of wealth to these two sources. Their estimate is about 30 percent, however, for those with incomes over $300,000.

It is not easy to accept these findings that accessions played only a small role in current wealth (even for persons with incomes over $300,000) and that the allocation of some appreciation to the accessions made no appreciable difference. But there is not much other evidence from surveys. The major Federal Reserve Board survey mentioned earlier contained less explicit inheritance questions than the one just discussed and did not cover gifts at all.[43] Each respondent was asked in effect whether the family's inherited assets as a fraction of total assets was "none," "some," "small," or "substantial." The answers are summarized in table 1-2. Again, it is not clear what allowance, if any, was made by the respondents for the appreciation of inherited assets. Their interpretation of "small" and "substantial" is also difficult to assess. The table does show a fairly consistent positive relationship between the relative importance of inheritance and the wealth level itself. It also shows the significance of inheritance to be similarly related to income and age. But it is impossible to make any quantitative evaluation of this from the published information.[44]

The scarcity of relevant data and the importance of the inheritance issue have combined to tempt some scholars to make inferences from fragmentary evidence. For example, Lampman suggested a rough estimate of the overall effects of material intergenerational transfers in the 1922–53 interval. Lampman noted that his estimates showed a real rise in total personal wealth from $348 billion in 1922 to $821 billion in 1953 (at 1922 prices). He suggested that this increase be interpreted as represent-

43. Projector and Weiss, *Survey of Financial Characteristics of Consumers.*

44. The inheritance response was included as a dummy variable in a regression model explaining family wealth. The variable has the expected positive sign and is statistically highly significant, but the relative weight of inheritance still cannot be determined. The data underlying the Projector and Weiss report have been examined by John Bossons ("The Distribution of Assets among Individuals of Different Age and Wealth," in Raymond W. Goldsmith, ed., *Institutional Investors and Corporate Stock—A Background Study* [Columbia University Press for the National Bureau of Economic Research, 1973], pp. 394–428). His tabulations include two types of evidence on inheritance—wealth held in personal trust and the estimated value of inheritances from estates in probate. There is a breakdown by age and wealth class, but the many cells with zero entries and the erratic nature of the figures make interpretation difficult. The value of estates in probate at one point in time, however, may provide a basis for estimating the expected value of inheritance over a lifetime.

Table 1-2. Inherited Assets of Consumer Units in Relation to Total Assets, by Size of Wealth, Income, and Age of Head, December 31, 1962
Percent

			Inherited assets			
			Portion of total assets		Not	
Group characteristic	None	Some	Small	Sub-stantial	ascer-tained	All units
All units	83	16	12	5	*	100
Size of wealth (dollars)						
1–999	95	5	5	*	*	100
1,000–4,999	87	12	9	4	*	100
5,000–9,999	82	18	12	6	*	100
10,000–24,999	77	23	17	6	*	100
25,000–49,999	75	24	16	9	*	100
50,000–99,999	74	24	12	12	2	100
100,000–199,999	46	54	32	22	*	100
200,000–499,999	59	41	28	13	*	100
500,000 and over	39	59	24	34	2	100
1962 income (dollars)						
0–2,999	84	16	10	6	*	100
3,000–4,999	88	12	9	3	*	100
5,000–7,499	84	16	12	4	*	100
7,500–9,999	80	20	14	5	*	100
10,000–14,999	84	16	11	5	*	100
15,000–24,999	73	27	21	6	*	100
25,000–49,999	58	42	34	8	*	100
50,000–99,999	71	26	12	14	3	100
100,000 and over	31	66	9	57	2	100
Age of head (years)						
Under 35	91	9	8	1	*	100
35–44	87	13	9	3	*	100
45–54	83	17	12	4	*	100
55–64	75	24	17	7	1	100
65 and over	79	21	12	9	*	100

Source: Dorothy S. Projector and Gertrude S. Weiss, *Survey of Financial Characteristics of Consumers* (Board of Governors of the Federal Reserve System, 1966), p. 148.
* 0.5 or less.

ing the "accumulation of a generation" from the 1922 starting point. According to this interpretation about 42 percent (348/821) of the wealth in 1953 "may thus be said to have come into the hands of its current owners by transfer between generations in the form of bequest, gift, insurance proceeds, etc."[45] In other words, as of 1953, $348 billion is assumed to derive from tranfers and the rest from accumulation.

45. Lampman, *The Share of Top Wealth-holders*, p. 218.

Lampman's interpretation was clearly questionable. It would only be valid under very implausible assumptions, and there are counterexamples that readily invalidate it. For instance, if wealth had held steady at $348 billion over the entire 1922–53 interval, this would not necessarily imply that all or any part of the $348 billion was transferred to the "next generation." In keeping with the life-cycle hypothesis, the dissaving of the retired population could be offsetting the saving of the working population, without any intergenerational transfers at all. Even the actual growth of wealth to $821 billion could be consistent with a total absence of inheritance. On the other hand, Lampman's interpretation could also understate the role of inheritance. Part of the real growth over the 31 years was that of inherited assets. As pointed out earlier, such accumulation is more appropriately viewed as a consequence of inheritance than of independent activity by the heir to the original bequest.

In a more recent analysis of Lampman's estimates and of Internal Revenue Service data, Lebergott attempts to demonstrate a prevalence of upward mobility and the creation of a nouveau riche even larger than suggested in the *Fortune* articles.[46] For example, Lebergott uses mortality rates to estimate the number of the top wealthholders in 1922 who survived until 1953.[47] He considers persons at least 71 years of age among the top wealthholders in 1953, assuming that they "consist only of survivors of the rich in 1922 plus recruits from those in lower wealth classes in 1922."[48] Estimating that there were 62,000 survivors from this top group in 1953 among the total of 255,000 estimated by Lampman, he concludes that the 193,000 residual (76 percent) were newcomers or nouveau riche.[49]

There are various levels of objection to Lebergott's reasoning, but perhaps the most fundamental is that many of these newcomers are the children of the original group who were rich in 1922. Even though 40 years of age or more, they may not yet have inherited wealth or, even if they had, the amount could have been insufficient to propel them into the 1922 estate tax returns. As individual wealth grew with age and inflation,

46. Lebergott, *The American Economy,* especially pp. 166–67.

47. "Top wealthholders" covers those appearing in the estate tax return data with a gross estate of $50,000 or more in 1922 and $60,000 or more in 1953 and 1969.

48. Lebergott, *The American Economy,* p. 166. This assumption is dependent on the further implausible assumption that at age 40 or more in 1922 their inheritances would have been essentially completed.

49. Similar reasoning led to even higher estimates of the nouveau riche, one being that 85 percent among top wealthholders in 1969 who were 55 years old or more were in that category.

children of the estate tax return filers in 1922 who had not yet inherited or who had, say, only $40,000 could appear in large numbers 31 years later among the top wealthholders in 1953 with gross estates of $60,000 or more. It is difficult to regard them as nouveau riche, however.[50] They need only have increased their gross wealth from under $50,000 to $60,000 or more in 31 years to be classed as newcomers. There is one clear indication of the way in which the use of absolute dollar levels may be inflating the number of newcomers. The number of top wealthholders over 70 was reported to have grown from 255,000 in 1953 to 1,392,000 in 1969; thus, not surprisingly, the method finds many new rich. All in all, this approach seems capable of greatly exaggerating the number of new rich and overly discounting the role of inheritance in the generation of wealth.[51]

In addition to the various ad hoc attempts to appraise the role of inheritance discussed here, there have been several theoretical analyses— some accompanied by computer simulation of changes over time. Among these are the work of Sargan, Stiglitz, Pryor, Blinder, Atkinson, and Smith and coauthors.[52] These efforts utilize assumptions and models that inevitably oversimplify the complex process of intergenerational transfers. Some of this work is very elaborate, however, and could lead to practical conclusions if it were given more empirical content. Since the present emphasis is on the empirical evidence, these studies are not relied on here.

50. If the analysis were directed to the top 1 percent or some other stipulated rank in each year, the problem of omitted children of the wealthy would be less severe.

51. There are other problems with the Lebergott method. For example, most inheritances come from the second decedent parent, many of whom may not die until their offspring are 50 or 60 or more. On the other hand, it should also be noted that at least one bias in the approach somewhat understates the number of new rich. Some survivors from the 1922 group may not be present in 1953. Thus assuming all survivors are old rich understates the residual defined as new rich.

52. J. D. Sargan, "The Distribution of Wealth," *Econometrica*, vol. 25 (October 1957), pp. 568–90; J. E. Stiglitz, "Distribution of Income and Wealth Among Individuals," *Econometrica*, vol. 37 (July 1969), pp. 382–97; Frederic L. Pryor, "Simulation of the Impact of Social and Economic Institutions on the Size Distribution of Income and Wealth," *American Economic Review*, vol. 63 (March 1973), pp. 50–72; Alan S. Blinder, "A Model of Inherited Wealth," *Quarterly Journal of Economics*, vol. 87 (November 1973), pp. 608–26; A. B. Atkinson, "A Model of the Distribution of Wealth," Working Paper 123, Department of Economics (Massachusetts Institute of Technology, 1974; processed); and James D. Smith, Stephen D. Franklin, and Guy Orcutt, "The Intergenerational Transmission of Wealth: A Simulation Experiment" (prepared for the Conference of Research in Income and Wealth, National Bureau of Economic Research, Ann Arbor, 1974; volume forthcoming).

Scope of the Present Discussion

Having concluded that the miscellaneous ad hoc empirical speculations referred to above do not isolate the role of inheritance in the wealth
distribution, it is time to mention the three lines of research to be discussed in some detail below. Since all three investigations are speculative,
some potential alternative approaches are summed up in the appendix.

The first approach to be discussed below is an attempt to infer the role
of inheritance in the accumulation of wealth by using the distribution of
married women according to their net worth as a benchmark. It is argued
that these women derive the bulk of their wealth from intergenerational
transfers. The analysis leads to the speculation that half or more of the
wealth of moderately wealthy to very wealthy men can be attributed to
such transfers. But the validity of this speculation depends on a rather
subjective case concerning the inheritances of married women.

The next general line of investigation covers relevant aspects of the
life-cycle hypothesis, which has been invoked by some to suggest that
wealth inequality may be due in large part to the wealth-age relationship.
If true, wealth inequality would be a less urgent problem; if most inequality were due to age differentials, this would indicate no rigidity of
wealth ranks. In fact, this would represent almost complete equality on a
lifetime basis and no special advantage or disadvantage due to intergenerational transfers. This is not to suggest that inequality at a given time
is of no importance. With wealth goes power, and the variation of power
with age would be a continuing source of conflict, even if there were no inequality within age classes. In any case the latter appears to be far from
the truth. It will be shown that routine saving out of earnings could not
account for the great inequality of wealth. It will also be shown that great
inequality exists even among homogeneous age groups; although the implications of this are not as straightforward as they may first appear to be,
it is concluded that the reality of the wealth-age relationship does not succeed in seriously downgrading the role of inheritance in wealth-building.

Next to be considered is the literature relating the wealth of fathers
and sons. Of course, this relationship does not depict the role of inheritance explicitly. Many factors other than explicit material gifts and bequests underlie the correlation of the wealth of fathers and sons. Even so
it is useful to evaluate the closeness of this overall relationship as evidence

of the advantages or disadvantages of parental wealth as determinants of wealth levels attained by children.

Taken together, the findings add up to substantial evidence for the proposition that intergenerational influences—especially gifts and bequests—are a major force in the perpetuation of wealth inequality. Such influences of parents are generally beyond the control and volition of their children. Intergenerational transfers that enrich the younger generation generally do so without productive effort on the part of the latter.[53] Insofar as society desires to reduce wealth inequality and prefers to tax unearned rewards at relatively high rates, these findings have a clear policy implication. Moreover, apart from any effects via the bequest motive of the older generation, these transfers do not offer incentives to productivity. This suggests that more effective estate and gift taxation would reduce inequality with only minimal effects on productivity.[54]

53. This is not to deny the occasional existence of explicit or implicit quid pro quo requirements imposed on heirs.

54. Potential qualifications of this conclusion should be noted. Prospective estate and gift taxation could affect the behavior of a parent during the course of his life. If his gift and bequest motive is very strong, taxation of his planned transfers to heirs could have a substantial work disincentive effect, and he might also save much less. On the other hand, he might thwart gift and estate taxes by transferring more of his wealth to heirs in the form of human capital—investment in their education, for example—which would hardly be an unproductive consequence. In any case it seems unlikely that the prospect of transfer taxes far in the future has a powerful effect on the career behavior of the parent generation. Moreover, it is shown in chapter 3 that wealthy retired persons tend to continue accumulating wealth until death.

chapter two **Inheritance as a Determinant of Personal Wealth: Inferences from Data on Married Men and Women**

The object of this chapter is to evaluate the relative importance of intergenerational inheritance and independent accumulation in the building of personal wealth (interpreted here as a person's net worth). This can be studied directly for some persons, such as former Vice-President Nelson A. Rockefeller, who have made public their assets and inheritances. But no information is available to enable one to reach general conclusions—at least not directly. A direct approach to the question would require an expensive, large-scale statistical survey linking the wealth of individuals to gifts and inheritances received over their lifetimes. So in quest of a good first approximation, it is appropriate to turn to the official wealth estimates, even though they were developed for other purposes.

Substantial official information exists on estates, and some on intergenerational gifts, reported for federal and state tax purposes, but there is no evidence on how their disposition augmented relatively the wealth of heirs and donees. This aspect of the intergenerational transfer process is entirely below the surface.[1]

What is desired for specified wealth ranks is the ratio of wealth resulting from intergenerational transfers to total wealth, including any variations of this ratio by wealth rank. Given the information available and special advantages derived from distinguishing married male and female wealth distributions, it proved useful to break down this ratio into more measur-

1. Some states levy taxes on individual inheritances (rather than on estates), but there is no record of individual wealth at the time of each transfer, so there is no way of appraising the relative importance of such additions to a person's wealth.

able components. Denoting male and female wealth by M and F, wealth arising from intergenerational transfers by subscript i, and total wealth by subscript t, the desired ratio for married women is simply F_i/F_t. For married men the decomposed ratio is given by the identity

(1) $$M_i/M_t \equiv F_i/F_t \cdot F_t/M_t \cdot M_i/F_i.$$

Attempts to evaluate the three ratios on the right side of this expression will be reported in the next two sections. The clue that inspired the present analysis is provided by the contrast in the wealth-age relationship of male and female top wealthholders in the United States—that is, those persons in the living population who have gross wealth of more than $60,000, which is the estate tax exemption limit. The first hypothesis here was that the ratio F_i/F_t might be fairly close to 1. It grew out of the observation that in a given year male wealth is much more strongly related to age than female wealth is. In 1969, for example, among the top male wealthholders covered by data in an Internal Revenue Service report, wealth rose steadily with age; it averaged $63,000 for men under 40, compared with $218,000 for men aged 70 or over—a differential of 3.5 to 1. For women under 60 average wealth was virtually the same in each of the three age groups listed (under 40, 40 to 49, and 50 to 59)—about $171,000; then there was a gradual increase to $195,000 for women over 70.[2]

These contrasts in the wealth-age relationship led to speculation in the Internal Revenue Service report: "The pattern for women is not as closely correlated to age, probably owing to the way wealth is obtained." Added later was a corollary interpretation: "Most of the males who became top wealthholders probably accumulated most of their wealth, rather than acquired it through gift or inheritance."[3] This latter assumption concerning the relative role of accumulation and inheritance is debatable and indeed is the subject at hand; however, the implication that independent accumulation was of greater importance for men than women seems quite plausible.[4]

These considerations led to the hypotheses outlined below. They will be tested against official data on the wealth of the living and of decedents.

2. U.S. Internal Revenue Service, *Statistics of Income—1969, Personal Wealth Estimated from Estate Tax Returns* (Government Printing Office, 1973), p. 3.
    3. Ibid., pp. 3, 71.
    4. Since male top wealthholders are wealthier overall, this point does not imply that inheritance was any less important for them in *absolute terms* than for women.

Interpretation of these tests, however, will also require a statistical model for estimating the relative size of the bequests received by men and women.

Preliminary Hypotheses

The focus of the comparison between men and women can be sharpened by restricting it to married persons. It should be stressed that the emphasis is on the determinants of the relatively substantial wealthholdings found in the estate tax return data and described here as "top" wealthholdings. Indeed considerable attention will be given to persons with a net worth of over $100,000—the top 3 percent of married wealthholders in 1972. As a first approximation, it seems likely that the wealth of married women at this level is derived primarily from transfers from the previous generation and the appreciation of those transfers. The historic role of married women has virtually denied them the opportunity to accumulate substantial wealth in any other way; they are probably less likely than single women (who work with greater frequency) to have independent accumulations. Moreover, married women are unlikely to have inherited from previous husbands. A virtual lack of relationship between female wealth and age has already been noted in the 1969 data. This is consistent with a predominant role for inheritance in creating top wealthholders. Why are older women not substantially wealthier? These women are likely to have inherited their wealth earlier and in smaller amounts. Even though their wealth usually grows over time, it is not surprising to find it roughly equal to the more recently acquired wealth of younger women.

Table 2-1 portrays the wealth-age relationship in greater detail for married top wealthholders only and for the latest year available—1972. The married female wealth-age relationship was less flat in 1972 than for all women in 1969. After age 50, however, there is only a modest tendency for female wealth to rise in relation to age. On the other hand, male net worth in this same age range and upper wealth class more than doubles between the youngest and oldest age classes. Over the entire age range male net worth also rises fairly steadily from 49 percent of the female level to 122 percent. This pattern appears reasonably consistent with the hypothesis that wealthy married women attain their status primarily via intergenerational transfers, while the inherited wealth of men is substantially augmented by independent accumulation.

Table 2-1. Mean Net Worth of Married Top Wealthholders, by Age and Sex, 1972[a]

| Age | Net worth (thousands of dollars) | | Male net worth as percent of female net worth |
	Male	Female	
Under 40	52.2	107.0	49
40–49	103.6	151.5	68
50–54	124.8	180.9	69
55–59	167.7	176.9	95
60–64	180.7	178.7	101
65–69	211.7	205.5	103
70–74	226.2	211.6	107
75–79	240.6	173.2	139
80–84	234.2	201.6	116
85 and over	266.0	214.0	122

Source: U.S. Internal Revenue Service, *Statistics of Income—1972, Personal Wealth Estimated from Estate Tax Returns* (Government Printing Office, 1976), pp. 37, 39. These estimates of the wealth of the living are derived from estate tax returns by the "estate tax multiplier" method based on mortality rates. For a discussion of the rates and method used, see ibid., pp. 59–60. For a more detailed description, see Robert J. Lampman, *The Share of Top Wealth-Holders in National Wealth, 1922–56* (Princeton University Press for the National Bureau of Economic Research, 1962), chap. 2.
a. Top wealthholders are those with gross assets of over $60,000.

It may be surprising to note in table 2-1 that among top wealthholders under 60 in 1972, women have greater average wealth than men. But this indicates greater wealth inequality among women than men, rather than greater wealthholdings by *all* women under 60.[5] Consider the persons under 40 years of age. Women in this age group who attained top wealth-holder status had twice the average wealth of men. But this does not mean that *all* women under 40 were wealthier on the average than men in this age class. Nearly three times as many men as women were to be found in this top wealth group, and the total assets of the women were only about $81 billion, compared with $127 billion for the men.[6]

Plausible hypotheses explaining these wealth-age relationships are (1) that most of the female minority in this wealth class reached it via inheritance; and (2) that the higher mean for young women in this class, indicating greater inequality among the women, suggests a greater inequality of inheritances than among other independently accumulated wealth-

5. For example, the Pareto measure of inequality for a high open-ended class is determined solely by the relation of the mean in that class to the lower limit. See R. G. D. Allen, *Mathematical Analysis for Economists* (St. Martin's, 1969), p. 408.
6. Among those in the top wealthholder class were an estimated 1.635 million men and 0.580 million women with mean total assets of about $78,000 and $139,000, respectively; the net worth means were $52,000 and $107,000, respectively. (For source, see table 2-1.)

holdings. In keeping with the original hypothesis, the male majority, while also inheriting, is apparently aided much more by relatively modest independent accumulation in attaining the top wealth class. Although the men are bunched closer to the lower limit of the class, they are still wealthier as a group because there are many more of them.

In short, the greater average wealth of the female minority in the top wealth class among persons under 60 does not indicate that these women are wealthier than men under 60. At the same time, the evidence is entirely consistent with the hypothetical contrast in the mode of accumulation by the two sexes. For this age range only, it is also consistent with a corollary hypothesis to be discussed later—that wealth *inequality* is greater among women.[7] This latter finding for younger women is essentially equivalent to that of Harbury and Hitchens for the United Kingdom: "Wealth distribution tends to be more unequal among women than among men and inequality is greatest among lower age-groups for female wealth holders."[8]

Potential avenues to great wealth, other than transfers from prior generations, are not likely to have been rewarding to married women. Transfers from husbands and independent accumulation are the main potential qualifications of this generalization and should be considered in turn. Transfers from living husbands can occur through the assignment of joint ownership or via outright gifts from husband to wife. Neither route seems likely to add substantially to the wealth of wives.

First, holding property jointly does not appear to be a major means of transfer. The official estimates of the distribution of personal wealth of the living population are built up from the estates of decedents. Insofar as the jointly held property of decedent wives can be shown to have been acquired by their husbands' funds, that portion of the property will generally be excluded from their estates and from the corresponding estimates of the wealth of living married women in their age class.[9]

7. It should be mentioned that the ratios of wealth means given in the last column of table 2-1 offer a comparison of male and female *inequality* by age class and not a comparison of wealth *levels* by sex. Thus it offers mixed evidence on the hypothesis that inequality is greater among women. For age classes over 60, inequality among top wealthholders appears greater among men. In other words the positive relation between inequality and age is stronger for men, suggesting that variations in independent accumulation build up the inequality caused by inheritance.

8. C. D. Harbury and D. M. W. N. Hitchens, "Women, Wealth and Inheritance," *Economic Journal*, vol. 87 (March 1977), p. 124.

9. It is true, of course, that the executor must show that jointly owned property with the right of survivorship did not originate with the decedent. The value of the

The exclusion from the wife's estate of jointly held property derived from the husband's funds is not complete, however. In the case of community property states, the wife's estate may include what are effectively transfers from her husband. In California, Texas, and six much less populous states all property acquired by either spouse is owned by them separately but in equal shares. If, for example, all property actually derived from the husband's earnings, but the wife died first, half of its value would appear in the wife's federal estate tax return. But in California in the late sixties, for example, about 80 percent of estates contained separate property only, and only 5 percent had community property only.[10] Although community property was more prominent in large estates, the inclusion of these transfers appears to inject only a minor bias, especially when it is recognized that community property rules cover only about one-fifth of the nation's population.

Outright inter vivos gifts from the current husband are, of course, not excluded from the wife's estate, but the potential magnitude of such gifts also seems small. The latest gift tax statistics show total gifts of $4 billion in 1965. The marital deduction totaled only $150 million, indicating that $300 million was claimed by donors as gifts to spouses.[11] Gifts are small relative to intergenerational bequests. For example, in 1965 reported "distributable estates" totaled $10 billion, after deducting bequests to spouses and charitable contributions. Even allowing for some intragenerational transfers, the $300 million in gifts to spouses seems relatively small—perhaps 4 percent of the magnitude of intergenerational transfers.[12]

---

property is taxable in the estate "unless the executor submits facts sufficient to show that the property was not acquired entirely with consideration furnished by the decedent, or was acquired by the decedent and the other joint owner or owners by gift, bequest, devise, or inheritance" (Internal Revenue Regulation 20.2040-1(a), cited in David Westfall, *Estate Planning Problems* [Foundation Press, 1973], p. 258). Although the burden of proof appears to be on the executor, it should not be difficult in the case, say, of a jointly owned home—especially if the wife had no substantial independent income.

10. State Controller, Inheritance and Gift Tax Division, "Statistics of California State Inheritance Tax, Fiscal Years Ended June 30, 1967, and June 30, 1968" (Sacramento: January 1970; processed), p. C-24.

11. U.S. Internal Revenue Service, *Statistics of Income—1965, Fiduciary, Gift, and Estate Tax Returns* (GPO, 1967), p. 49.

12. Ibid., pp. 60–61. All these figures understate the actual totals because of nonfiling when small amounts are involved, incomplete use of the potential deduction, and so on. The 4 percent estimate seems fairly reliable, however.

Another indication that the importance of inter vivos gifts from husband to wife is small, especially in recent years, is provided by evidence collected by the Treasury Department. For example, decedents in 1959 with estates in the $1 million to $3 million range were found to have transferred only 5–8 percent of their assets during life.[13] It is also likely that much of this amount went to beneficiaries other than wives. Further evidence of sparse utilization of the gift process as a tax-saving device is the evidence presented in chapter 3 that the wealth of wealthy men usually grows rapidly up to the time of retirement and continues to grow more slowly after that. This would be difficult to accomplish if large inter vivos gifts were simultaneously depleting the wealth of those men.

Another potential source of wealth of the married female decedent not deriving from prior generations is transfers from a previous husband. In keeping with the discussion above, it is assumed that these take the form primarily of bequests to widows from previous husbands (rather than inter vivos transfers). It is difficult to even guess the importance of such bequests, but only married female decedents who were previously widowed could owe any of their wealth to this source.[14] Obviously the probability that a decedent falls in this category varies directly, and presumably strongly, with age. The fact that the wealth of decedent wives does not rise substantially with age suggests that this is probably a minor source of their wealth.

Finally, a married woman is also unlikely to have achieved substantial independent accumulation. As defined earlier, the only two forms of independent accumulation are (1) saving out of earnings and the going rate of return on it; and (2) extraordinary entrepreneurial and investment returns—that is, returns on capital above the going rate. Although there is a trend toward greater labor force participation by women, the frequency and duration of their employment and their rate of compensation are still substantially lower than for men. Moreover, among the older age ranges where most of the wealth of married women is to be found, the past work force participation and earnings of these older women was clearly much lower than for the younger women of today. Evidence on saving out of earnings may be sought in a comparison of the wealth distributions of single and married women. The official figures show that the former are

13. Joseph A. Pechman, *Federal Tax Policy* (3d ed., Brookings Institution, 1977), pp. 231–32.
14. No way of estimating the fraction of decedents who fit this description appears to be available.

generally much wealthier—about as wealthy as married men.[15] Unfortunately these surprisingly high wealth levels for single women indicate only that they fare better than married women. If the single women, who work much more, were not much wealthier, this would have implied that saving had a minor role in wealth-building for both groups of women.[16]

The opportunity for highly successful entrepreneurship or extraordinary return on other types of investment would seem especially uncommon for married women. There is evidence, at the very high wealth levels at least, that women have rarely accomplished such accumulation—certainly far less often than men. The three surveys of multimillionaires in *Fortune* magazine found no women who had become ultra rich except through inheritance.[17] In 1957 an estimated 64 men and 12 women had fortunes of over $75 million. Among these, 35 men were reported to have "made their fortunes on their own," but none of the women had done so.[18] The survey in 1968 found 54 men and 12 women with wealth over $150 million. Half of the 12 women were not among the previous 12, but again all 12 on the 1968 list owed their great wealth to inheritance. The survey implied that more than 30 of the men made the list on their own. Finally, the 1973 *Fortune* list reported 39 new rich, but no women were among them.

This indication of the small role of independent accumulation in the generation of the wealth of wealthy women is supported by the survey of women in the United Kingdom by Harbury and Hitchens: "Wedgwood's

15. For example, consider the three major age classes studied later. For married women in the 55–64, 65–74, and 75-and-over age classes in 1972 the percentage whose net worth was over $100,000 was about 4.00, 4.49, and 5.06, respectively. The corresponding estimates for single women were 8.60, 9.25, and 12.94. (For source and method, see table 2-1.)

16. With respect to their opportunities for wealth accumulation, single and married women also differ in two other presumably smaller and offsetting ways. Single women have a greater chance of accumulation via entrepreneurship, but only married women can benefit from transfers from current and past husbands. It is of course possible that single women inherit more due to greater need, although results from the inheritance model to be discussed later did not show need to be a factor in the size of bequests.

17. Richard Austin Smith, "The Fifty-Million-Dollar Man," *Fortune,* November 1957, pp. 176 ff.; Arthur M. Louis, "America's Centimillionaires," ibid., May 1968, pp. 152 ff.; and Arthur M. Louis, "The New Rich of the Seventies," ibid., September 1973, pp. 170 ff.

18. Smith, "Fifty-Million-Dollar Man," p. 177. As stated in chapter 1, although the fortunes of these 35 men grew rapidly, it is misleading to say all were self-made. Many, such as J. Paul Getty, had sizable inheritances or substantial financial backing from their fathers.

observations on the sources of women's property in the 1920s remain valid: only a very small minority of women (no more than 5%) accumulated their wealth through what is generally regarded as 'entrepreneurship'."[19]

In sum, it seems safe to assume that substantial wealthholdings among married women are primarily created by gifts and bequests from prior generations and the normal growth of these funds over time. Transfers from earlier and current husbands and independent accumulation were probably of second-order importance. This does not mean, however, that transfers were of the same relative importance at all levels of the wealth distribution. Indeed the second hypothesis here is that in the case of married men especially, the higher the wealth level, the greater the relative importance of intergenerational transfers.

It is probably extremely rare that a person can save enough from earnings to accumulate a very large fortune. Such fortunes are almost certainly generated primarily through inheritance or exceptionally successful investment. On the other hand, in the case of the median wealth level of around $15,000 in 1977, it seems plausible that a fairly substantial part of this would typically be generated by saving out of earnings.[20] More generally, the hypothesis is that the higher the wealth rank, the less the relative importance of accumulation out of earnings and therefore of the overall role of both types of independent accumulation.

The two general hypotheses of this section are:

1. The wealth of top wealthholders among married women is generated primarily from intergenerational transfers; these women therefore will usually have less wealth than men who not only inherit but also benefit from greater independent accumulation.

2. The relative role of independent accumulation is less, the higher the wealth rank; since men do most of the independent accumulation, this makes for relatively lower wealth differentials in favor of men over women

19. Harbury and Hitchens, "Women, Wealth and Inheritance," p. 8. See also Josiah Wedgwood, *The Economics of Inheritance* (London: Routledge, 1929; Kennekat, 1971).

20. This rough estimate of median wealth is derived from Dorothy S. Projector and Gertrude S. Weiss, *Survey of Financial Characteristics of Consumers* (Board of Governors of the Federal Reserve System, 1966), p. 96. The median net worth on December 31, 1962, was put at $6,700 (by interpolation). On the basis of 1962–72 gains by wealth ranks, as illustrated later in table 2-2, the ten-year rise in wealth was put at about 75 percent, suggesting (after 15 years) a 1977 median of around $15,000.

in the higher ranks (and less inequality among men). These two general propositions are illustrated by the hypothetical Pareto lines in figure 2-1. Since men not only inherit but also accomplish the bulk of independent accumulation, their cumulative wealth distribution line is to the right of that for women. The assumed lower relative differential in favor of men at higher wealth levels is portrayed by the steeper line for men, representing a less unequal wealth distribution.[21]

Empirical Evidence

The hypothesized relationship between the wealth distributions of married males and females displayed in figure 2-1 was checked against the official net worth distributions. Formally, this means only that the data were examined for evidence that the Pareto line for husbands was to the right of and steeper than that for wives. It must be stressed that a formal finding to this effect is a necessary but insufficient condition to show that the *substance* of the hypotheses is true. The substance was that the wealth of wives was primarily derived through transfers from prior generations and therefore was less than that of husbands who can achieve greater independent accumulation; moreover, the role of intergenerational transfers in the wealth of husbands is relatively greater the higher the wealth rank. An empirical confirmation of the configuration in figure 2-1 would be consistent with these hypotheses, but that pattern could conceivably be accomplished in other ways. After the empirical findings are reported, alternative interpretations of their implications for hypotheses 1 and 2 will be considered.

Cumulative personal wealth distributions of the type sketched in figure 2-1 were estimated from Internal Revenue Service reports and summarized in table 2-2. For appropriate comparisons of male and female wealth, the data were interpolated to obtain the wealth levels corresponding to specified ranks (measured in percentiles from the top).[22]

21. A corollary hypothesis is that single women have somewhat more independent accumulation than married women but far less than married men. Such a pattern was flatly ruled out, however, by the 1972 data reported earlier. Despite presumably lesser earnings and fewer entrepreneurial opportunities, single women appear just about as wealthy as married men. It is possible that the latter inherit less; more likely, they accumulate less due to family responsibilities.

22. Percentiles were used rather than the more conventional measurement of the shares of the top 1 percent, 2 percent, and so on. The former utilized the reliable estimates of the total number of persons, but the latter would have depended on questionable estimates of aggregate wealth throughout the entire range.

**Figure 2-1. Hypothetical Cumulative Wealth Distributions of
Married Men and Women**

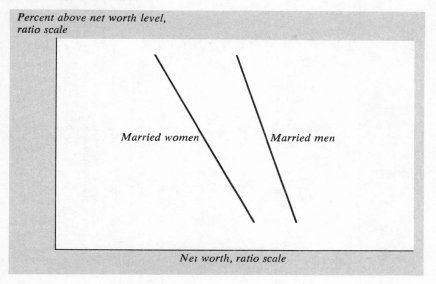

*Percent above net worth level,
ratio scale*

Married women   *Married men*

Net worth, ratio scale

Consider first the 1969 data that were the source of the Internal Revenue Service conjectures leading to the present hypotheses. The lowest reliable comparison is for husbands and wives ranking (in net worth) 2 percent from the top in their own distributions. The data for that rank confirm the lower wealth of women at $85,000, compared with $150,000 for men, or a female-male ratio of 57 percent. The lower wealth of women is found at all the specified ranks through the 0.01 percent level—the cut-off point for the top 1 in 10,000 in each wealth distribution. The wealth of men at this rank is estimated to be $4.25 million, compared with $3.35 million for women at the same relative position in their own wealth distribution.[23] This result is consistent with hypothesis 1 and is found in all three years and at all ranks.

Hypothesis 2 is also supported by the 1969 figures. The relative differential between men and women is substantially greater at the lower levels. In terms of figure 2-1, this supports the steeper slope (less inequality) in the male than in the female distribution.[24] In the lowest three

23. Since the number of married men is assumed to be equal to that of married women (47.24 million), this refers to the 4,724th person in each distribution.

24. It should be repeated that these empirical findings *consistent with* hypotheses 1 and 2 are necessary but not sufficient conditions for their validity.

Table 2-2. Net Worth Percentile Ranking of Married Males and Females, 1962, 1969, and 1972[a]

Net worth in thousands of dollars; ratios in percent

Percentile rank (from top)	Net worth, 1962			Net worth, 1969			Net worth, 1972		
	Male	Female	Ratio, female to male	Male	Female	Ratio, female to male	Male	Female	Ratio, female to male
3.00	...	...	...	114	...	...	126	73	58
2.00	97	...	...	150	85	57	166	97	58
1.00	157	87	55	245	137	56	271	158	58
0.50	250	140	56	386	221	57	427	253	59
0.20	460	294	64	680	435	64	800	505	63
0.10	710	505	71	1,040	740	71	1,260	790	63
0.05	1,100	780	71	1,590	1,210	76	1,940	1,210	62
0.02	1,970	1,440	73	2,780	2,160	78	3,410	2,010	59
0.01	3,170	2,240	71	4,250	3,350	79	5,250	2,950	56

Sources: U.S. Internal Revenue Service, *Statistics of Income—1962, Personal Wealth Estimated from Estate Tax Returns* (Government Printing Office, 1967), pp. 22–23; ibid., *1969* (GPO, 1973), pp. 22–23; ibid., *1972* (GPO, 1976), pp. 15–16; U.S. Bureau of the Census, *Statistical Abstract of the United States, 1963* (GPO, 1963), p. 36, and issues for 1970, p. 32, and 1973, p. 38.

a. Percentage cumulative frequency distributions of wealth ranked from the top were derived from the official 1962, 1969, and 1972 personal wealth estimates. These were based on total married population estimates. (The total number of married men was consistently slightly lower than that of married women because of exclusion of some members of the armed forces. Thus the total for women was used—43.85 million in 1962, 47.24 million in 1969, and 49.05 million in 1972.) The selected percentiles in this table were estimated by algebraic linear interpolation after the double logarithmic Pareto-type transformations. That is, a linear relationship was assumed between the logarithm of the percentage cumulative frequency and the logarithm of net worth in the range above $80,000. This relationship appeared linear enough above net worth of $80,000 for this interpolation to be adequate and reliable, except for the one portion of the data noted in the text. No estimates were made for net worth levels substantially below $80,000. Not only did the linearity break down, but the official estimates of frequencies are likely to be low, even for classes slightly above the exemption. For example, some gross estates in the $60,000–$80,000 range are rendered nontaxable by exemptions and deductions, and returns may not have been filed.

ranks tabulated, the wealth of women was found to be 56–57 percent of that of men, while in the top three ranks women fared relatively better with 76–79 percent of the net worth of men. Assuming that inheritances dominate the female distribution and are distributed similarly among males, this tends to confirm that the importance of inheritance is relatively greater at higher levels of the male distribution.[25] The same pattern was found somewhat less strongly in 1962 when this female-male ratio was 55–56 percent for the two lowest ranks, compared with 71–73 percent in the top four ranks.

The 1972 figures do not generally confirm the tendency for women to fare better relative to men in the higher ranks. The ratio rises irregularly from 58 percent at the rank of 3 percent from the top to 63 percent at the 0.2 and 0.1 percent ranks, but it drops back to an average of 58 percent at the top two ranks. It should be noted, however, that the official estimates are suspect in the two highest ranks of the married female distribution in 1972. For example, the official estimates show a decline of 25 percent in 1969–72 in the number of women with a net worth of over $5 million; the number for 1972 in the class interval immediately below that also appears to be an underestimate.[26] But even allowing for these potential underestimates, it appears that the support for hypothesis 2 is much weaker in 1972 than in the two earlier years.

In view of the peculiarities described, it would be useful to have some basis for evaluating the potential error in these personal wealth distribution estimates. The sampling error in the original selection of estates is not a serious problem. Those over $300,000 were sampled at a 100 percent rate, and the 157,000 other estates were sampled at a 20 percent rate.

25. Male and female inheritance patterns are compared empirically in the next section.
26. The estimates show a drop in the number of married women with wealth over $5 million from 2,500 in 1969 to 1,900 in 1972. Estimates in this range are of course based on a very small number of decedents, but at least the number of decedents in this top class did rise from 15 to 24. This seeming contradiction is apparently due to a difference in the age distributions in the two years. Even so, the results for this wealthy class seem implausible for a three-year interval in which the wealth of women in the $100,000–$1 million ranks gained around 15 percent and the wealth of men in the top rank gained more than 20 percent. The estimates for the $1 million–$5 million married female class are similarly questionable, even though the basic data on decedents appears sufficient and plausible. The number of decedents rose 40 percent, from 184 to 257, but the estimated number of living wealthholders in this class rose only 10 percent. This low estimate may be compared with the number of living males in that class, which also showed a 40 percent increase. In short, the last two estimates in the last two columns of table 2-2 seem much too low.

Table 2-3. Estimated Wealth Distributions Based on Data for Married Persons with Net Worth over $100,000, by Age and Sex, 1962 and 1972

Year and age group	Male					Female					Ratio of female to male percentiles (percent)		
	Percent with net worth above $100,000[a]	Slope of Pareto line[b]	Percentile[c] (millions of dollars)			Percent with net worth above $100,000[a]	Slope of Pareto line[b]	Percentile[c] (millions of dollars)					
			1	0.1	0.01			1	0.1	0.01	1	0.1	0.01
1962													
Total	1.93	1.535	0.153	0.69	3.08	0.83	1.461	0.088	0.426	2.05	58	62	67
55–64	4.06	1.553	0.246	1.09	4.78	1.75	1.420	0.148	0.751	3.80	60	69	79
65–74	4.56	1.551	0.265	1.17	5.18	1.86	1.502	0.151	0.700	3.24	57	60	63
75 and over	4.51	1.440	0.284	1.41	6.97	1.93	1.421	0.159	0.803	4.05	56	57	58
1972													
Total	4.18	1.528	0.255	1.15	5.19	1.90	1.524	0.152	0.690	3.12	60	60	60
55–64	7.93	1.521	0.390	1.77	8.06	4.00	1.541	0.246	1.095	4.88	63	62	60
65–74	9.72	1.479	0.465	2.14	10.47	4.49	1.476	0.276	1.316	6.26	59	61	60
75 and over	8.96	1.430	0.463	2.32	11.60	5.06	1.618	0.272	1.130	4.64	59	49	40

Sources: U.S. Internal Revenue Service, *Statistics of Income—1962, Personal Wealth Estimated from Estate Tax Returns* (Government Printing Office, 1967), pp. 48, 50; and ibid., *1972*, pp. 43, 45.

a. Frequencies and aggregates were adjusted relatively for unknown ages so that sum of frequencies and aggregates over all age groups equaled totals for all ages. (Total for all males is set equal to total for all females.)

b. This slope is negative. Absolute value (a) derived from $\overline{NW} = [a/(a-1)]$ ($100,000), where $\overline{NW}$ is mean net worth over $100,000. (See R. G. D. Allen, *Mathematical Analysis for Economists* [St. Martin's, 1969], p. 408.)

c. These percentiles were derived algebraically from each line determined by the percent above $100,000 and the tabulated slope of the Pareto line.

The questionable estimates appear in the high ranges where all estates were included in the analysis.[27] The potential error is primarily due to the existence of only a very small number of estates in some top wealth classes, especially those for women. Only small samples of decedents are available for inferences concerning the wealth of the living. Not only do these estates often represent small samples of the living, but the mortality rates used are difficult to evaluate—especially their variation by wealth level. There appears to be no objective way of appraising these estimates.[28]

Since age has substantial effects on wealth, it seemed appropriate to examine homogeneous age groups separately. The only useful available information by age, sex, and marital status is that giving the number of persons with a net worth of over $100,000 and their aggregate net worth.[29] These data for married persons above the net worth level of $100,000 are sufficient for estimating the wealth distribution in its approximately linear range.[30] Pareto lines were estimated for the aggregate distribution and three wealth-age classes for the years 1962 and 1972, and results based on this exercise are displayed in table 2-3.[31]

The percentage of all married men whose net worth was above $100,000 is substantially higher than for women. This is consistent with table 2-2, but here the wealth advantage of men is shown to be equally true of homogeneous age groups as well. For both years the percentage of men with wealth over $100,000 is roughly double the ratio found for women. A better comparison is available for given ranks among the male and female distributions. For this purpose three percentiles—1, 0.1, and

27. Internal Revenue Service, *Statistics of Income—1972*, p. 60.

28. For a discussion of the statistical methodology used, see ibid., pp. 59–60.

29. Similar information is available for persons whose net worth is over $60,000, but this is not reliable. The minimum requirement for filing estate tax returns is a gross estate of $60,000, but it is likely that returns for a substantial number of estates somewhat larger than that are never filed. After exemptions and deductions, many of these estates would owe no tax. This could also result in the omission of an appreciable number of estates with net worth over $60,000. The shape of the distributions appears to support this conjecture. In any case this problem caused by nonfilers probably is virtually nonexistent for estates with a net worth over $100,000.

30. The cumulative distributions are approximately linear after the logarithmic transformation, as in figure 2-1. Pareto lines such as those illustrated in figure 2-1 can be approximated by a single point (given by the percentage frequency above $100,000) and the slope derivable from the mean net worth above that level. (See Allen, *Mathematical Analysis for Economists*, pp. 407–08.)

31. For these three classes, total population estimates were available without interpolation.

0.01—were estimated.[32] The most stable pattern was found for the first percentile. The female-male ratio for all married persons at this rank rose from 58 to 60 between 1962 and 1972; the results for age groups varied little from the aggregate, and the 1972 ratios were correspondingly higher by two or three percentage points in each group. This suggests that the age breakdown essentially confirms the 58 and 60 percent female-male wealth ratios at this rank. The ratios at other ranks showing consistently lower wealth for women are also consistent with hypothesis 1.

Once again in table 2-3 the evidence for hypothesis 2 is mixed but weaker than that in table 2-2. In 1962 the Pareto lines for males were steeper in all age groups. Correspondingly, the female-male ratios in table 2-3 rise with wealth rank, again indicating greater inequality among women than men. This female-male contrast in the degree of inequality varies with age and is somewhat less in the aggregate than shown in table 2-2. The Pareto slopes for men and women are very nearly equal in the aggregate and for the first two age groups in 1972. The ratios for these groups also confirm table 2-2 in showing little variation with wealth rank that year. The estimates for persons 75 years of age and over are the reverse of hypothesis 2, suggesting less inequality (steeper slope) among women than men. As in the case of table 2-2, however, irregularities in the estimates for wealthy women tend to discount this result.[33]

It is appropriate to recall as a qualification the evidence for 1972 in table 2-1. Those data covered all gross estates above $60,000. For reasons already mentioned, data on wealth classes below $100,000 are less reliable. Moreover, the linearity of the Pareto lines breaks down in the $60,000–$100,000 range. Even so, it should be repeated that table 2-1

32. Each of the 16 Pareto lines derived for this table was based on one point, at the $100,000 level, and the aggregate net worth of wealthholders above that level. This is a slender reed on which to base the percentile estimates. However, a comparison of the aggregate results in this table with those derived from the more detailed information available in constructing table 2-2 inspires some confidence. The first percentiles here in thousands of dollars for 1962 and 1972 are 153 and 255 for men, and 88 and 152 for women. These algebraic estimates check well against the corresponding interpolations in table 2-2: 157 and 271 for men and 87 and 158 for women—a maximum difference of 6 percent. The two sets of eight higher percentiles agree almost as well in relative terms, although there is one discrepancy of 15 percent (the 0.1 percentile for women in 1962). The comparison of men and women may be more reliable than this suggests, since the same linear approximation has been used for both.

33. For example, the mean net worth in this group is reported to have declined from $337,000 to $262,000 between 1962 and 1972. This is presumably due to the implausibly low 1972 estimates for very wealthy women, as discussed earlier.

shows the mean wealth for women under 60 greater than that for men. This suggests that for age groups lower than those available in table 2-3, inequality may be substantially greater among women than among men, as originally hypothesized.[34] However, the rough estimates derivable from the means in table 2-1 suggest that, if anything, inequality among older men is greater than among women of the same age. This is in accord with the questionable results in table 2-3 for persons over 75. If valid, this would suggest that independent accumulation by males over a lifetime generates ultimate inequality among older persons greater than that due to inheritance alone.

In sum, the breakdown of the wealth of the living by age in table 2-3 strongly confirms the wealth differential in favor of married men over women. But the hypothesized variation of this advantage with wealth level is rather weakly supported by the evidence for 1962 and not at all by that for 1972. The less reliable figures of table 2-1 do support this hypothesis (equivalent to greater inequality among women) for persons under 60 but show the opposite for older persons. One is left with a firm conclusion that men are wealthier than women in all age classes—a finding consistent with the hypothesis that men achieve substantially greater independent accumulation. Evidence for the hypothesis that inheritance plays a relatively larger role in male wealth at the higher wealth levels remains mixed.

Since irregularities are apparent in the estimates of the wealth of the living based on decedents' wealth, it is appropriate to ask what may be learned from the wealth distribution of the decedents themselves. Unfortunately after 1961 the official vital statistics reports no longer break down total decedents by marital status. Reliable estimates can be developed for 1962, however, and are reported in table 2-4, along with more speculative estimates for 1972.

A comparison of percentiles in table 2-4 with those in table 2-2 shows both male and female decedents to be roughly half again as wealthy as living wealthholders in these top ranks. At the same time, the new estimates confirm the relative lag of female wealth behind male wealth rank by rank. In addition, the analysis of decedents for 1962 confirms the earlier finding in showing the female-male wealth ratio to be positively related to wealth rank. This ratio for decedents rises from 48 percent to 69 per-

34. For the relationship between means in a top class and the Pareto inequality measure, see table 2-3, note b.

Table 2-4. Net Worth Percentile Ranking of Married Male and Female Decedents, 1962 and 1972[a]

Net worth in thousands of dollars; ratios in percent

Percentile rank (from top)	Net worth, 1962			Net worth, 1972		
	Male	Female	Ratio, female to male	Male	Female	Ratio, female to male
3.00	110	. . .	. . .	182	101	55
2.00	148	. . .	. . .	244	132	54
1.00	248	120	48	399	208	52
0.50	387	194	50	649	330	51
0.20	705	389	55	1,195	617	52
0.10	1,105	645	58	1,820	1,005	55
0.05	1,750	1,075	62	2,770	1,580	57
0.02	3,210	2,045	64	4,820	2,880	60
0.01	4,690	3,220	69	7,340	4,530	62

Sources: U.S. Internal Revenue Service, *Statistics of Income—1962, Personal Wealth Estimated from Estate Tax Returns* (Government Printing Office, 1967), pp. 22–23, and ibid., *1972*, pp. 15–16; and U.S. Public Health Service, *Vital Statistics of the United States, 1961*, vol. 2, pt. A (PHS, 1964), table 5-5.

a. The estimation method was the same as that described in table 2-2 except that estimates were required of the total number of married male and female decedents in 1962 and 1972. These were obtained from the total number of decedents in each year by applying (for males and females separately) the fractions who were married in 1961. (For an evaluation of the 1972 estimates, see text.) Consequently in 1962 the number of females used was 94,473 multiplied by a correction factor of 0.3215. The number of males used was 92,117 multiplied by a correction factor of 0.5718. In 1972 the figure used for males was 1,096,000 (same correction factor as above) and the figure used for females was 867,000 (same correction factor as above).

cent between the 1.00 and 0.01 percentiles.[35] Despite irregularities in between, this overall differential is quite consistent with the 55 to 71 range in the estimates for the living. So the data for decedents confirm the indicated greater inequality among women and the implied greater relative importance of inheritance in the higher male wealth ranks in 1962.[36]

The estimation of percentiles for decedents in 1972 is hampered by the absence of a current breakdown by marital status. The proportions in 1961 can be used for crude estimates. Even though these percentiles themselves are unreliable, the resulting *slopes* of the Pareto lines illustrated in figure

35. The 69 percent ratio for the highest percentile is a weak estimate due to the small number of female decedents on which it is based. The 64 percent ratio for the 0.02 percentile is fairly solid, however, based primarily on 52 estates worth more than $2 million.

36. The rise in the ratio with wealth rank is equivalent to a steeper Pareto line for women, as illustrated in figure 2-1. Insofar as the female distribution reflects primarily inheritance and the male inheritance experience is similar, the narrower female-male gap among the higher ranks implies a greater role of inheritance relative to independent accumulation, the higher the male wealth rank.

2-1 are independent of these crudely estimated totals. As a result, the *ratio* of female to male percentiles is virtually independent of the totals assumed.[37] So it is possible to reliably test whether the second hypothesis predicts a steeper slope (less inequality) in the male wealth distribution.

Unlike the case in 1962, the female-male ratios for decedents in 1972 in table 2-4 are substantially different from the results for the living in table 2-2. After a decline in the ratio from 55 to 51 percent, the figures for decedents show a steady rise to 62 percent. The earlier 1972 results for the living showed a rise from 58 to 63 percent and then declined to 56 percent in the high wealth range—apparently casting doubt on hypothesis 2. But it is significant that the data for decedents, on which the estimates for the living are based, support the hypothesis from the 0.5 percentile on up.[38] Although the female-male ratio for decedents declined slightly in the first few percentiles listed, the overall effect is to give some slight support to hypothesis 2; however, the evidence here is much less strong than that recorded for 1962.

In sum, all the empirical evidence strongly indicates a substantial wealth differential against married women relative to men; this is at least consistent with hypothesis 1. The 1962 data for decedents also confirm that the earlier results for the living are consistent with hypothesis 2, predicting a steeper Pareto line (less inequality) in the male net worth distribution. The 1972 data on decedents tend to refute the earlier results based on the derivative wealth distribution of the living population and add modest support for hypothesis 2.

The empirical findings reported above covered only formal features of the wealth distribution of married men and women. Relative to the figures for women, male wealth was found to be consistently higher, and there was also some less solid evidence of less inequality among men. The implications of these results for an evaluation of the role of inheritance in perpetuating the inequality of wealth require further consideration. One of the essential ingredients is a comparison of inheritance by men and women.

37. Insofar as the Pareto plots depart from linearity these ratios are not completely independent of the estimated totals. These plots are remarkably linear for decedents in the wealth range over $100,000, however. Thus the estimated ratios are virtually insensitive to moderate variations in the estimated totals.

38. The contrasting results for decedents are consistent with the doubts expressed earlier concerning the upper tail of the estimated wealth distribution in 1972 for living females; the estimated numbers in the top two classes appeared much too small in light of the data on decedents.

A Simple Model of the Determinants of Inheritance

If it is true that the wealth of wealthy married women is generated primarily by intergenerational transfers, what are the implications of the previous comparisons of male and female wealth distributions for an evaluation of the role of inheritance in generating the fortunes of married men? If, other things being equal, men and women tend to inherit equally, the excess of male net worth over female net worth at each rank can be attributed to independent accumulation by married men. On the other hand, if men tend to inherit more, as may be the case with the very wealthy, only a part of the excess of male wealth over female wealth can be attributed to independent accumulation. For this reason, estimating the role of inheritance requires a comparison of the inheritances accruing to men and women.

Data were available on the inheritances received by sons and daughters of a sample of persons who died in the Cleveland area in 1964–65.[39] After an inventory of the available information, a simple multiplicative model was devised to measure the relative propensities of men and women to inherit.[40]

The base from which bequests flow is the decedent's estate. The gross size of the estate was included in the model as the primary explanatory variable.[41] The share of the estate bequeathed to an individual (son and daughter) was then assumed to be inversely proportional to the number of children in the family. Finally, a dummy variable was included in this basic model to estimate any differential in the other-things-equal inheritance propensities of sons and daughters. The variables in the model are

INHER = inheritance in thousands of dollars (since an inheritance listed as zero actually implies a bequest from zero up to $500, such observations were taken to be $250);

39. These data were generously made available by Marvin B. Sussman, Judith N. Cates, and David T. Smith, authors of *The Family and Inheritance* (Russell Sage Foundation, 1970).

40. The earlier inheritance concepts discussed above included gifts by the living. In the present analysis the concept of inheritance is confined to bequests, since no information on gifts is available. It seems likely, however, that any favoritism existing in bequests, such as a larger share to sons, would also characterize the pattern of inter vivos gifts.

41. Net estate size was also derivable, but the results for gross estates are reported here, since the fit was slightly better for that variant, and the coefficients differed minimally.

SHARE = fraction of childrens' total inheritance accruing to an individual son or daughter under equal division (reciprocal of number of children);

GRST = gross estate in thousands of dollars;

SEXDUM = dummy variable representing sex = zero for son, one for daughter.

The simple model for the estimation of the determinants of inheritance is

(2) $$INHER = a\ SHARE^b \cdot GRST^c \cdot d^{SEXDUM}.$$

For consistency with the previous analysis the model was applied to *married* sons and daughters only. It was assumed that children of the decedent inherited the lion's share of the estate only if the decedent had no living spouse as a potential heir. Indeed it seems likely that the bulk of intergenerational bequests are received from the second decedent parent (plus smaller amounts from divorced first decedent parents). So the model was fitted first to the data for unmarried decedent parents. After the logarithmic transformation, the regression result (with standard errors in parentheses) was

(3) $\log INHER$ = 0.188 + 0.838 log $SHARE$
(0.122) (0.137)

+0.663 log $GRST$ −0.036 $SEXDUM$
(0.072) (0.666)

$n = 192;\ \bar{R}^2 = 0.406.$

The coefficients (elasticities) from the share and estate size variables are highly significant with the expected sign.[42] The simple model explains about 41 percent of the variation in individual inheritances.

Most important for present purposes is the insignificance of the −0.036 coefficient on the sex dummy measuring the differential between sons and daughters. This implies that given the size of family and gross estate, bequests to sons tend to average 109 percent of bequests to daughters. Since the small deviation of this ratio from 100 percent does not approach sta-

42. The coefficient for gross estate is significantly less than 1, indicating that a given relative differential in the size of two estates is generally accompanied by a somewhat smaller relative differential in predicted bequests. This could be due in part to a tendency for children to inherit smaller portions of large estates; for example, bequests to other relatives and charitable contributions may increase relatively with estate size. The share elasticity is not significantly less than 1, suggesting, ceteris paribus, that the relative share of each individual child in the total bequests to children is apt to be that predicted under equal distribution.

tistical significance, the data reveal no favoring of sons in the bequest decision. In other words, no discriminatory bequest behavior such as primogeniture appears to have favored sons—at least not in this across-the-board wealth distribution of Cleveland decedents in 1964–65.[43]

Next to be considered are bequests to sons and daughters by married decedents. These were expected to be much smaller, with a large portion of the estate going to the surviving spouse. The fitted equation for this group is

$$(4) \quad \log INHER = -0.411 + 0.308 \log SHARE$$
$$ (0.100) \quad (0.111)$$

$$+0.283\ GRST\ -0.105 \log SEXDUM$$
$$(0.066) (0.050)$$
$$n = 279;\ \bar{R}^2 = 0.104.$$

For these data on married decedents (who undoubtedly bequeath substantial amounts to their spouses), it is not surprising to find a very poor fit and much lower coefficients (elasticities) for the share and estate size variables than for unmarried decedents. Bequests by the married decedents to their children are much more erratic and much less sensitive to the share and estate size constraints. It is surprising, therefore, to find a significant coefficient for the dummy variable distinguishing sex. The estimate indicates a tendency for a son to inherit 127 percent of the amount inherited by a daughter whose married decedent parent has the same gross estate and the same number of children (as in the case of brothers and sisters). Although this male-female differential is significant (at the 5 percent level), it appears much less important in practice than the finding of no significant difference between sons and daughters of unmarried decedents. This follows from a comparison of the magnitude of inheritances by children in the two data sets.

Data for these 1964–65 decedents show a crudely estimated median inheritance of $2,900 for children of unmarried decedents, compared with $500 in the case of married decedents.[44] This is a substantial difference

43. Taken together, this evidence plus the nearly unitary elasticity of the share variable are consistent with the hypothesis of generally equal division among all children, regardless of sex or age rank. A correlation of bequest size with age rank is not completely ruled out, however.

44. These are very crude estimates, since they depend on the mean of the logarithm of inheritance and assume symmetry in the distribution of these logarithms. Both (especially the second) are likely to be overestimates due to clustering at the low end of the inheritance distribution even after the logarithmic transformation. (The figures cited are actually harmonic means.)

given that the more accurately estimated median estate sizes were rather close for the two classes of decedents at $12,800 and $11,200, respectively.

The $2,900 median inheritance and $12,800 estate characterizing the first group seem plausible given the mean of 3.9 children per family.[45] On the other hand inheritances by the sons and daughters of married decedents are very small, as expected.

How can the evidence be summed up? There is an indication of some sex discrimination in the generally small bequests by the first decedent parent, but little sign of it in the much larger bequests by the second decedent parent. One approach is to combine the data, while adding to the model a dummy variable representing marital status of the decedent. The latter is enormously significant with a t ratio of 18; the coefficient (0.770) implies that, with the share, estate size, and children's sex variables held constant, bequests by unmarried decedents to their children tend to be six times those by married decedents. In this combined sample and generalized model the dummy variable distinguishing sons and daughters is just barely significant.[46] It implies that sons tend to inherit 119 percent of the amount inherited by daughters.

Despite the last finding, it seems reasonable to conclude that these data suggest a somewhat smaller discrimination in favor of sons.[47] The bulk of inheritance is derived from unmarried decedents and the indicated discrimination in the other smaller bequests carries less weight. It should be stressed, however, that these results are derived from the full range of this particular wealth distribution sample. Among the very wealthy, the picture may be quite different, as suggested by the *Fortune* surveys discussed earlier. They find only 15 to 20 percent as many women as men among those who owe their great wealth primarily to inheritance.[48] Perhaps the safest conclusion is that sons fare as well as or better than

45. This high average family size is due partly to the demographic characteristics of the Cleveland area, but also to the fact that a family was included in the present analysis only if at least one son or daughter existed and cooperated with the interviewers.

46. The coefficient (-0.0749) carries a t ratio of 1.81 and is significant at the 5 percent level on the one-tail test.

47. Attempts to generalize the model were unsuccessful and did not alter the picture presented here. For example, "need" for bequests indicated by the prebequest economic status of the son and daughter was tested but found to have no influence. This is again consistent with generally equal division among siblings.

48. One example of this contrast is the large inheritance of John D. Rockefeller, Jr., relative to the amounts bequeathed in trust to his sisters.

daughters. There is only marginal evidence that sons do better generally, but there are considerably stronger indications that they are luckier when it comes to inheriting great fortunes.

Interpretation and Tentative Conclusions

In the context of the approach adopted here, it would be possible to derive a clear picture of the role of intergenerational transfers in the generation of wealth (net worth) levels at various ranks among married men and women if three ratios were accurately measured at selected ranks. These are the three ratios on the right of identity 1 given at the start of this chapter. In order of their discussion, these are the ratios: F_i/F_t, female wealth generated by intergenerational transfers to total female wealth; F_t/M_t, total female wealth to total male wealth; and M_i/F_i, male wealth generated by transfers to female wealth generated by transfers. The relative weight of intergenerational transfers in female wealth is given quite directly by F_i/F_t. For married men the appropriate ratio is given by the product of the three ratios.

Although better indications of the three component ratios have been obtained than of the ultimately desired ratio for men, the range of potential error was still substantial. In such circumstances it may be useful to specify two alternative estimates for each. Although this process is subjective, the purpose is to set down ranges that seem likely to include the true value in each case. Since some evidence was reported showing that the relative importance of inheritance increases with the wealth level (especially in the case of males), these ranges will be specified separately for the 2.00 percentile and the 0.01 percentile.

The ratio F_i/F_t is essential to the estimates for both men and women. Unfortunately it is the least measurable of all. It was argued above that this ratio might be fairly close to unity—almost certainly closer than the corresponding ratio for men. This argument entailed a downgrading of the following potential generators of the wealth of wives: (1) the assignment of joint ownership to wealth actually accumulated by husbands; (2) outright gifts from husbands to wives; (3) transfers to these women from previous husbands—especially decedent husbands; and (4) independent accumulation by wives. On the basis of a priori reasoning and casual empiricism these were all assumed to be of minor importance. In this spirit one may guess that this ratio is between 65 and 85 percent at the 2.00 percentile and between 70 and 90 percent at the 0.01 percentile.

Alternative empirical estimates of the female-male total wealth ratio F_t/M_t were derived earlier. Estimates for the lower rank fell in the range 55–60, and those for the higher rank were in the 60–80 range except for several aberrations due to suspect estimates of personal wealth in the two highest classes for wives in 1972.[49] Discounting the latter, and taking the other results (based on the official figures) at face value, these two ranges will be assumed for this ratio.

The ratio M_i/F_i relating the wealth of married men generated by intergenerational transfers to the female wealth so generated was estimated by regression fitted to the full range of the wealth distribution. Point estimates of this ratio were obtained ranging from 109 to 127 percent. These are subject to sampling error, however; the high figure also carries less weight, since it was based on the very small inheritances from married decedents. On the other hand, these across-the-board estimates may be too low if assigned to the 2.00 percentile. Given these conflicting biases, the range was put at 100–120 percent for this rank; at least the lower limit of 100 percent seems plausible, since no hypothesis or empirical finding suggests that women usually inherit more than men. Since other studies showed much less frequent inheritance of very great fortunes by women than by men, this range was raised to 110–130 percent at the 0.01 percentile.

The results of these quasi-empirical estimates are summarized in table 2-5. Only the result for the middle ratio relating total female and male wealth has a fairly solid empirical foundation. The last ratio is based in part on regression analysis but is subject to sampling error and weakened by a largely inappropriate range of observation. The first ratio (indicating the role of intergenerational inheritance in the wealth of wives) is almost pure guesswork. Even so, it is interesting to ask what M_i/M_t ratio is implied by the product of several sets of three percentages. For example, if the midpoint of each interval were correct, this would imply that 47 percent of male net worth at the 2.00 percentile (about $165,000 in the 1972 distribution for living husbands) is accounted for by intergenerational transfers. The corresponding figure for the 0.01 percentile ($5.2 million in 1972) is 67 percent. These figures refer, of course, not to any

49. As suggested above, the wealth of married women appears to have been substantially underestimated in these classes.

**Table 2-5. Estimates of Ranges that Include Specified Wealth Ratios at
Alternative Percentiles**
Percent

	Percentile	
Ratio[a]	2.00	0.01
F_i/F_t	65–85	70–90
F_t/M_t	55–60	60–80
M_i/F_i	100–120	110–130

Source: See text.

a. F_t and M_t equal female and male wealth, respectively, generated by intergenerational transfers; F_t and M_t equal total female and total male wealth, respectively.

single wealthholder at a given net worth rank, but rather to the aggregate weight of inheritance among a number of persons in the vicinity of that rank.

If the percentage representing the assumed weaker appraisal of the role of inheritance indicated by each ratio (the lower end of the specified range) is adopted in this exercise, the role of inheritance in male wealth is 37 percent at the lower rank and 46 percent at the higher rank. The corresponding figures based on the upper end of all three ranges are 61 percent and 94 percent, respectively.

The alternative male inheritance ratios are presented here, not as estimates, but as the implication of alternative plausible values of the three component ratios—plausible on the basis of the previous discussion. Despite the varying reliability of the underlying component ratios in table 2-5, however, these speculative male inheritance ratios cannot be readily dismissed. The lowest figure cited above (37 percent) is a good illustration. The 55 percent component for F_t/M_t has solid empirical support. The 100 percent figure for M_i/F_i is a plausible lower limit, since no one has suggested that men inherit less than women. Only the 65 percent figure for the role of inheritance in the wealth of decedent wives is sheer guesswork. If it is accepted, 37 percent would be the conservative estimate of the role of inheritance in the wealth of living married males of all ages at the $165,000 level in 1972.[50] On the other hand, if the 65 percent F_i/F_t figure (and only that one among the three) could be shown to be exaggerated, the 37 percent inheritance would have to be revised downward in proportion to the ratio of the true lower figure to 65 percent.

50. It should be noted that the 37 percent figure applies also to decedents, who tend to be older and wealthier; for example, the 2.00 percentile for male decedents was $244,000 in 1972 (table 2-4), compared with $166,000 for living males (table 2-2).

On the basis of all the foregoing surmises and estimates, the 37 percent role for inheritance at the $165,000 male wealth level seems a highly conservative lower limit. On the other hand, the maximum listed role for inheritance of 94 percent seems implausibly high, even at the male wealth level of over $5 million in 1972. So, like its opposite number, this seems to be a highly conservative upper limit—almost certainly an overstatement.[51]

Finally, a word should be said about the more plausible intermediate ratios of 47 percent and 67 percent for the role of male inheritance at the male net worth levels of $165,000 and $5.2 million, respectively. The *Fortune* surveys concluded that only half of the ultra rich achieved their wealth via inheritance. This might suggest that the 67 percent intermediate inheritance figure at the $5.2 million level is an exaggeration. But the *Fortune* classification of the wealthy into two categories—inherited and self-made—may be misleading. For example, J. Paul Getty's fortune was put at $700 million to $1 billion in 1957 when he was 65 years old, and it was *not* classified as inherited.[52] Yet Getty is reported to have inherited one-half million dollars; perhaps more important, he has described how his early wildcatting ventures were fully financed by his father, as some kind of silent partner.[53] An appraisal of the extent to which his 1957 fortune was inherited requires knowledge of the timing of these transfers from his father, what he already had when they were received, and Getty's own long-run rate of return on his capital. For example, if he put up none of the original investment and earned only an average rate of return, the entire fortune should be regarded as inherited.[54] Of course, if he earned an extraordinary rate of return, it would seem reasonable to credit him with some independent accumulation even if he put up nothing. In any case, only a careful analysis could tell whether or not his inheritance and earlier financial backing was of primary importance in the building of Getty's fortune. More facts are needed, but it would be absurd to look at

51. The 90 percent and 80 percent extreme components seem most vulnerable here; the latter figure (for F_t/M_t) in particular was an extreme value found only for the distributions of the living men and women in 1969.

52. Smith, "Fifty-Million Dollar Man," p. 177.

53. J. Paul Getty, *How to Be Rich* (Playboy Press, 1966), p. 5.

54. The average rate of return was very high when Getty was accumulating his fortune. For example, one estimate shows the real rate of return on industrial equity (based on Moody's price indexes for industrial common stocks) was 9 percent in the 1919–65 interval. (John A. Brittain, *The Payroll Tax for Social Security* [Brookings Institution, 1972], p. 163.)

the original value of his inheritance and say that Getty inherited less than one-tenth of 1 percent of his fortune.

The evidence and reasoning here have pointed to intergenerational transfers as a major instrument in the building of fortunes and, therefore, the perpetuation of the inequality. It is recognized, however, that these conclusions are critically dependent on largely a priori reasoning asserting a dominant role for such transfers in the accumulation of wealth by married women. The two other major areas of empirical work on this question —the estimation of the wealth-age relationship and the father-son wealth relationship are taken up in the next two chapters.

chapter three **The Implications of the Life-Cycle Hypothesis and the Wealth-Age Association**

The evaluation in chapter 2 of the weight of inter-generational transfers in the building of personal wealth is rather speculative. Against it should be set a newly prominent invocation of the life-cycle hypothesis—one that has been reported extensively by the Royal Commission on the Distribution of Income and Wealth.[1] Nothing said here will explicitly and directly demonstrate the importance of inheritance; rather, the attempt will be to "back into" the answer. The question is whether the wealth-age association is a major alternative explanation of the inequality of wealth observed in a given year. The finding is that even though this association is strong, it explains only a small part of the observed degree of the inequality of wealth. The implication by default is that the major sources of inequality are to be found elsewhere—in gifts and bequests and occasional extraordinary yields on venture capital.

An editorial in the London *Times* nearly a decade ago tried to downgrade the importance of inheritance as a cause of wealth inequality. It did so by asserting that the life-cycle pattern of saving was a major cause.

Quite obviously in the most egalitarian of societies one would not expect the new-born babe and the man on the point of retirement to have identical savings, or even the fifty-year-old and the sixty-year-old, and there must therefore be a concentration of wealth in a minority of hands in any society one can conceive of.[2]

1. See Royal Commission on the Distribution of Income and Wealth, *Initial Report on the Standing Reference,* Report 1, Cmnd. 6171 (London: Her Majesty's Stationery Office, 1975), pp. 110–17.
2. *Times* (London), September 28, 1968, cited in A. B. Atkinson, "The Distribution of Wealth and the Individual Life-cycle," *Oxford Economic Papers,* n.s., vol. 23 (July 1971), p. 240.

In response Atkinson sought to show that this argument does not have the quantitative significance attributed to it.[3] Even so, the wealth-age relationship as an explanation of wealth inequality was given a fresh start and is still challenging the older view that inheritance is the key factor.

If the *Times* were right in its emphasis, the inequality of wealth at a given moment would not be of great importance. The implication was that wealth inequality is a relatively benign phenomenon—one that does not cause or reflect vertical socioeconomic immobility. The rich, who are likely to be elderly, are where they are, not because of special advantage or extraordinary accumulation, but because they have saved for a long time. The poor, who are likely to be young, will have their day. If this argument ever prevailed, it would mean that the advantages or disadvantages of birth had been dismissed as major causes of the inequality of wealth.[4]

The *Times* editorial invokes in effect one tenet of the neoclassical life-cycle hypothesis discussed earlier.[5] It assumes an upward trend of individual wealth with age but does not assume the drawing down of wealth upon retirement. The editorial added an empirical point, suggesting that "in the most egalitarian society over 80 percent of the total private wealth would be in the hands of men over 50 who would comprise less than 15 percent of the population." No source is given, and it is difficult to accept the interpretation. If the estimates are based on the actual wealth share of men over 50, this empirical point does not demonstrate what would be found "in the most egalitarian society." Moreover, these data do nothing to explain why the top 1 percent tend to hold around a quarter or more of all wealth in the United Kingdom and the United States.

Quasi-Empirical Analysis of Life-Cycle Factors

Atkinson's original rebuttal began with a hypothetical question: If everyone were identical except for age, and if gifts and bequests were prohibited, how much wealth inequality would there be as the result of

3. Atkinson, ibid., pp. 239–54.
4. This does not imply that wealth inequality among age groups at a given time is of no social importance. The concentration of wealth (and power) in the hands of the older generation could well create social tension and accentuate the generation gap.
5. See, for example, Franco Modigliani and Richard Brumberg, "Utility Analysis and the Consumption Function: An Interpretation of Cross-Section Data," in Kenneth K. Kurihara, ed., *Post Keynesian Economics* (Rutgers University Press, 1954).

age differences alone? Lacking explicit data on inheritance, his tactic was to ask whether, in a world without intergenerational transfers, the observed degree of inequality could possibly be generated by life-cycle behavior.[6] In other words, he sought to establish the role of inheritance by default—that is, by proving that life-cycle factors could not cause the observed inequality and thus implying that something else must be responsible. Atkinson's analysis downgraded the importance of a life cycle of saving as a factor in wealth inequality and evoked many responses. It may be useful to review the controversy in some detail and to add some U.S. data to the picture. In its most general form, the life-cycle hypothesis simply asserts that personal wealth is systematically related to the age of the individual. The key point in the present context is that even if everyone had the same earnings and no inheritances took place, persons of different ages would have accumulated various amounts of wealth. This would happen even if there were no differences in wealth among people of the same age.

The life-cycle hypothesis assumes that people save in order to provide for some planned pattern of consumption over their lifetimes. There are great variations in such plans relating to individual preferences, the earnings-age relationship of the individual, and uncertainty about the future. Despite this high variability the life-cycle hypothesis is widely assumed to explain the pattern of personal saving—especially the provision for retirement, including contributions to pension programs.[7] Recently this hypothesized lifetime saving pattern has been put forward as a benign factor underlying the inequality of wealth.

How much does routine lifetime saving have to do with the observed inequality? At the a priori level the controversy has involved successive

6. Atkinson's work on the life cycle was followed by a more general analysis in the same vein leading to the conclusion that routine saving out of earnings could not account for great fortunes. Therefore these could only be generated by inheritance and extraordinary accumulation or capital gains. See A. B. Atkinson, *Unequal Shares: Wealth in Britain* (London: Penguin, 1972), chap. 3.

7. The discussion of the life-cycle explanation of saving and wealth has been most active in Britain, but the need to include pensions in the analysis has been stressed recently by Feldstein in this country. He argues that the wealth-age profile is more in tune with the prediction based on the life-cycle theory of saving if accrued pension claims are included in wealth. Undoubtedly the saving and dissaving associated with accumulation and consumption of pension claims is the best example of the assumed life-cycle behavior. See, for example, Martin Feldstein, "Social Security and the Distribution of Wealth," *Journal of the American Statistical Association*, vol. 71 (December 1976), especially pp. 800 and 806.

approximations. Atkinson began with explicit stylized models of individual saving behavior in order to appraise its importance in causing the wealth inequality that can be observed at any given time. His pioneer work underlies the lucid analysis and extensions in the Royal Commission report.

The first illustration, or stylized model, starts with the assumptions that everyone has the same life expectancy, the *same lifetime earnings,* and the same tastes. Everyone knows how long he will live and, while working, saves just enough for retirement. The Modigliani-Brumberg model assumes also that the rate of interest and the growth rate of earnings, consumption, and population are all zero.[8] For example, suppose each person works for 40 years (from age 20 to 60) and lives ten more years in retirement. Everyone earns $15,000 a year throughout his career and desires to consume the same amount each year, including the ten years of retirement.[9] In order to do this he must save a fifth of his income—$3,000 a year. After working 40 years, he will have accumulated $120,000 (without benefit of interest), allowing him to retire with a $12,000 annual consumption—the same as that enjoyed during the 40 working years. This particular life-cycle hypothesis produces for all individuals the wealth-age relationship in figure 3-1.

Since the saving habits of all individuals are identical in this illustration, the overall relationship of wealth to age will be the same as that sketched.[10] It can be shown that in such a distribution the top x percent of the population owns $x(200-x)/100$ percent of all wealth. So the top 1 percent of the population would have about 2 percent of total wealth, and the top 10 percent would have 19 percent. Since it is known that the top 1 percent own about one-quarter of the wealth in the United States, the wealth-age relationship depicted in this figure does not come close to explaining the observed degree of inequality. Obviously this first model is extremely unrealistic. Can more realistic assumptions about the wealth-age relationship go further toward an explanation of the distribution of wealth?

Atkinson's first generalization of the Modigliani-Brumberg model introduced positive real rates of interest and plausible rates of growth of

8. Modigliani and Brumberg, "Utility Analysis."

9. Obviously it is also assumed that there is no inflation and that the $15,000 is a constant real income.

10. Apparently the age distribution is also assumed to be uniform.

Figure 3-1. Hypothetical Wealth-Age Profile: I

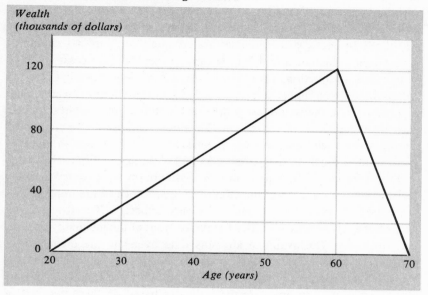

earnings, consumption and population.[11] He found that this had only a small effect on the predicted share of the top wealth ranks. It raised the shares by about one-half at most—with the predicted share of the top 1 percent going up to about 3 percent. He also tested the effect of using actual survival rates and more realistic income profiles (rising and then falling with age), but again there was little effect on the predicted shares. Account was also taken of the fact that not all adults can accumulate wealth out of earnings. Women who work as unpaid housewives cannot accumulate wealth out of earnings. The assumption that there is one such woman for every two working adults raises the shares of top ranks among potential wealthholders, but only by 50 percent. So even these modified models fall far short of explaining the actual inequality of wealth.

These largely a priori speculations, along with the empirical analysis discussed later, tend to discount the importance of life cycle factors in the distribution of wealth. Witnesses before the Royal Commission protested, however, that the equal-earnings assumption in these models causes an understatement of the role of the life-cycle in explaining the distribution

11. Atkinson, "The Distribution of Wealth," pp. 241–42.

of wealth. "In the real world, different individuals have different levels of earnings and such inequality in earnings, combined with life-cycle savings behaviour, will act as a powerful force towards concentration of wealth."[12] In effect, such witnesses are arguing that figure 3-1 should be generalized to include a family of wealth-age profiles with great variation in the vertical direction, as in figure 3-2. Persons with very high earnings will attain a much higher wealth peak before beginning to consume their capital. That is, the wealthiest people will be those in the highest income class near their time of retirement. Thus even without intergenerational transfers (and without property income), the resulting wealth distribution would be much more unequal than that of the simple life-cycle model.

This critique of the equal earnings assumption is obviously entirely reasonable, but once again the empirical significance of the implied generalization is smaller than might have been expected. The Royal Commission reports a study that tries to take account of the inequality of post-tax earnings.[13] The available after-tax data overstate the inequality of earnings because the data include property income. Explicit data on earnings overstate inequality because they do not allow for the equalizing effect of taxation.[14] In any case the estimates based on these two sets of data were averaged. The incorporation of estimated earnings differentials into a life-cycle model yielded a prediction of a 5.5 percent share for the top 1 percent and a 16.5 percent share for the top 5 percent. Adding the further adjustment for married women (mentioned in chapter 2) yielded an 8.25 percent share for the top 1 percent and 24.75 percent for the top 5 percent of all wealthholders.

The Royal Commission then compared these hypothetical wealth shares to Atkinson's adjusted estimates for the mid-sixties of 21.7 percent and 41.0 percent for those two wealth ranks.[15] It was conceded that the hypothetical share of the top 1 percent based on the life-cycle model is still far short of the actual share—as estimated by Atkinson. The combined hypothetical share of the next 4 percent, however, was 16.5 percent, compared with Atkinson's 19.3 percent estimate for the real world. "This sug-

12. Royal Commission, *Initial Report*, p. 112.
13. Ibid., pp. 112–13.
14. Both sets of data also overstate inequality because of the inclusion of the variation of earnings within careers. (Persons with high earnings may not necessarily rank so high on a lifetime basis.) On the other hand, grouping individuals in a top class understates inequality in both cases.
15. Atkinson, "The Distribution of Wealth," p. 252. These estimates are adjusted to include accrued pension claims, which reduced the estimated degree of inequality.

Figure 3-2. Hypothetical Wealth-Age Profile: II

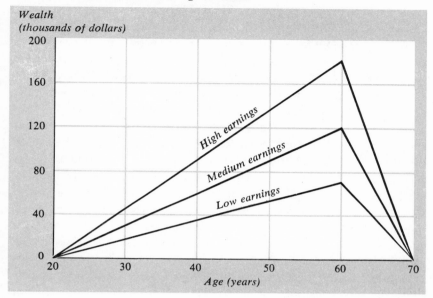

gests that the life-cycle theory may explain some of the inequality in the distribution of wealth, though it does not account for the heavy concentration of ownership in the top 1 per cent of wealth holders, where other factors, such as inheritance, play a more important role."[16]

These casual empirical invocations of the life-cycle hypothesis as a factor in the distribution of wealth are obviously very rough. But they generally support the hypotheses and statistical analyses based on U.S. data reported in chapter 2. It was suggested there that independent accumulation probably accounts for less than half of the wealth of the very wealthy for whom inheritance is a major factor; however, it was hypothesized that independent accumulation could be more important in the lower wealth ranks in the United States. Although such accumulation was not

16. Royal Commission, *Initial Report*, p. 113. Atkinson has suggested to me that the commission's evaluation of the explanatory power of the life-cycle hypothesis below the top 1 percent should be amended in one respect. After dropping the top 1 percent, the observed share of the next 4 percent should be expressed as a ratio to total wealth, excluding the inheritance by the top 1 percent. If the latter is taken to be the difference between the observed share of 21.7 percent and the hypothetical life-cycle share of 8.25 percent, the appropriate ratio is $19.3/(1 - 0.1345) = 22.3$ percent. This exceeds the hypothetical life-cycle share of 16.5 percent somewhat more significantly.

58   Inheritance and the Inequality of Material Wealth

found to be as important in the present study as suggested in the Royal
Commission report, its variation with wealth rank is worth stressing, since
it was noted in both analyses.

The emphasis on the variability of earnings as relevant to any tests of
the life-cycle hypothesis led to the detailed analysis of the question by
Oulton, who further generalized the analysis by Atkinson.[17] He too sought
to establish the importance of inheritance indirectly by downgrading the
significance of the wealth-age relationship in causing inequality.

Oulton, like Atkinson, began with a hypothetical economy without
intergenerational transfers. He asked what degree of wealth inequality
would be created by a lifetime cycle of saving, but he also allowed for the
effect of the inequality of earnings on saving. Oulton developed an elaborate model allowing for variations in the rate of interest and the growth
rate of earnings (due to work experience as well as economic growth).
The measure of wealth inequality adopted was the coefficient of variation
(ratio of standard deviation to mean). For a uniform earnings profile
across individuals, and various assumed values of the parameters in his
model, the maximum degree of inequality found was 0.6. When earnings
inequality was built into the model, the largest coefficient of variation
found was 0.9, even when estimated for the entire range of the working
life (18–65). He compared these to estimates of the coefficient of variation for actual wealth distributions. Even for homogeneous age groups
(ten-year intervals) these came to 4.0 or more—once again tending to
dismiss the life-cycle of saving as a major factor in wealth inequality.
Oulton then added a further refinement to his analysis—consideration of
the effects of variations across individuals in the rate of return on assets.
There was no evidence that such variation was sufficient to account for
the observed degree of inequality. To sum up, Oulton's generalization of
the model considered inequality of earnings and rates of return in addition
to age differences within the context of a life-cycle model. He concluded:
"The results indicate that none of these factors, either singly or in combi-
nation, are capable of accounting for a substantial proportion of actual
wealth inequality."[18]

Oulton mentioned three possible qualifications of his analysis that
caused him to hesitate before claiming a dominant role for inheritance.
The first two concerned the assumed pattern of saving behavior, but Oul-

17. Nicholas Oulton, "Inheritance and the Distribution of Wealth," *Oxford Economic Papers,* n.s., vol. 28 (March 1976), pp. 86–101.
18. Ibid., p. 99.

ton decided that his conclusions were not vulnerable on this score.[19] He was more concerned with a potential third objection that some individuals starting from a small capital base have accumulated large fortunes through entrepreneurial activity. Their initial capital may well have been borrowed or inherited, and their motives may have differed from those assumed in the life-cycle hypothesis. Insofar as they obtained extraordinary rates of return or capital gains, it seems appropriate to classify much of such wealth as independent accumulation. Oulton says there is no firm evidence on the quantitative importance of this type of accumulation, but he appears to concede that it may be a significant competitor to the weight assigned to intergenerational transfers. Thus he appears to accept the potential importance of the kind of super profits, gains, and windfalls stressed earlier by Atkinson and Thurow.[20] Even if many fortunes were initially accumulated in this way, this does not deny the importance of intergenerational transfers. It simply recognizes that extraordinary accumulation at one stage underlies many of the inherited fortunes.[21]

Evidence on Wealth Accumulation by U.S. Age Groups

This section is devoted to exploring whether U.S. data indicate a strong wealth-age relationship among wealthy persons. The stronger that relationship, the greater the role of age as a factor explaining the observed inequality. Also important is the shape of the wealth-age profile. In particular, what typically happens to wealth levels after retirement? This is relevant because if wealth then began to decline, a lesser role would be assigned to age in causing inequality. On the other hand, if wealth continued to rise after retirement that would suggest that inheritances and capital gains more than offset any dissaving out of current income.

Thurow has cited evidence on saving by age in the United States. By ten-year age classes, from age 25 on up to age 75 and over, the saving

19. Variation in the propensity to save (across individuals) would generate some inequality of wealth. It might be appropriate to give more attention to this factor.

20. Atkinson, *Unequal Shares,* chap. 3; and Lester C. Thurow, *Generating Inequality: Mechanisms of Distribution in the U.S. Economy* (Basic Books, 1975), chap. 6. For a comment on Oulton's analysis, see A. F. Shorrocks, *Oxford Economic Papers* (forthcoming).

21. This is not to say that routine accumulation out of earnings, as under the life-cycle hypothesis, can account for the great fortunes. As Atkinson and Thurow have said, these fortunes are too great to be derived in this way.

Table 3-1. Estimated Net Worth Percentiles for U.S. Male Age Cohorts, 1962 and 1972, and Growth Rates in Current and Deflated Dollars

Hundreds of thousands of dollars

Age in 1962	1962 percentiles[a]			1972 percentiles[a, b]			1972 as a percent of 1962			Annual percentage rate of increase			Real annual percentage rate of increase[c]		
	0.5	1.0	2.0	0.5	1.0	2.0	0.5	1.0	2.0	0.5	1.0	2.0	0.5	1.0	2.0
40–49	1.93	1.24	0.80	5.06	3.28	2.07	262	265	259	10.1	10.2	9.9	6.7	6.8	6.5
50–54	2.73	1.77	1.15	5.78	3.85	2.45	212	218	213	7.8	8.1	7.8	4.4	4.6	4.4
55–59	3.49	2.24	1.43	6.68	4.21	2.66	191	188	186	6.7	6.5	6.4	3.3	3.2	3.0
60–64	3.89	2.50	1.60	7.00	4.38	2.74	180	175	171	6.1	5.8	5.5	2.7	2.4	2.2
65–69	4.04	2.61	1.69	7.06	4.37	2.70	175	167	160	5.7	5.3	4.8	2.4	2.0	1.5
70–74	3.80	2.42	1.53	6.89	4.28	2.66	181	177	174	6.1	5.8	5.7	2.8	2.5	2.4
75 and over	4.35	2.70	1.68	8.42	5.12	3.11	194	190	185	6.8	6.6	6.4	3.4	3.3	3.0
All ages	1.65	1.06	0.67	3.18	2.02	1.28	193	191	191	6.8	6.7	6.7	3.4	3.3	3.3

Sources: U.S. Internal Revenue Service, *Statistics of Income—1962, Personal Wealth Estimated from Estate Tax Returns* (Government Printing Office, 1967), pp. 22–23; ibid., *1969* (GPO, 1973); pp. 22–23; ibid., *1972* (GPO, 1976), pp. 15–16; U.S. Bureau of the Census, *Statistical Abstract of the United States, 1963* (GPO, 1963), p. 36, and issues for 1970, p. 32, and 1973, p. 38.

a. Estimated by double logarithmic interpolation of Pareto function. For method, see table 2-2, note a. Population estimates by age class are from U.S. Bureau of the Census, *Current Population Reports*, series P-25, no. 519, "Estimates of the Population of the United States, by Age, Sex, and Race, April 1, 1960 to July 1, 1973" (GPO, 1974).

b. These are percentiles for the surviving individuals from each 1962 age cohort ten years later.

c. Net worth percentiles were deflated by consumer price indexes of 90.9 for 1962 and 125.3 for 1972 (1967 = 100).

rate (including capital gains and losses) was remarkably stable at around 30 percent.[22] No decumulation point is apparent in this cross-sectional survey; it suggests that people continue saving up to the time of death rather than beginning to dissave upon retirement. It is possible that elderly people continue to save for security, power, and bequest motives and, in some cases, owing to a decline in consumption with age. It should be mentioned, however, that survey data are often unreliable and that such a cross-sectional analysis would in any case be less valid than tracking the saving behavior of age cohorts through time.[23]

The absence of dissaving upon retirement is generally confirmed by the U.S. data on personal wealth by age. As table 2-1 showed, the wealth of a cross section of individuals—especially men—is positively related to age. It is possible to demonstrate this point even more strongly with the aid of time series data for age cohorts. The U.S. net worth distributions for 1962 and 1972 permit an analysis of wealth accumulation by given age cohorts over this ten-year interval. The persons in a given age cohort are essentially the same in 1962 and 1972 except for attrition due to death.[24] Table 3-1 presents estimated net worth percentiles for U.S. males in these two years. Their interpretation can be illustrated by the first entry at the upper left. It is an estimate that 0.5 percent of all U.S. males in the age class 40–49 in 1962 had a net worth of over $193,000. Then the 1972 percentile indicates that among the survivors of this same age cohort— age class 50–59 in 1972—0.5 percent had a net worth over $506,000.[25]

Table 3-1 offers a number of useful indications. For example, it con-

22. Thurow, *Generating Inequality*, p. 137. Thurow based his study on the Survey of Consumer Expenditures, 1960–61, conducted by the U.S. Bureau of Labor Statistics and reported in BLS, *Consumer Expenditures and Income, Total United States, Urban and Rural, 1960–61*, Report 237-93 (BLS, February 1965).

23. Although these survey data on savings fall short of more accurately estimated national aggregates, the direction of any bias introduced by this shortfall is not apparent.

24. They are not precisely identical, because the population statistics exclude citizens overseas. I am grateful to Gerald R. Jantscher for the suggestion that a ten-year comparison of age cohorts might be fruitful. For an analysis of British cohorts going back to 1923, see A. B. Atkinson and A. J. Harrison, *The Distribution of Personal Wealth in Britain* (Cambridge University Press, forthcoming), chap. 9. An earlier analysis of the British data is that of A. F. Shorrocks, "The Age-Wealth Relationship: A Cross-Section and Cohort Analysis," *Review of Economics and Statistics*, vol. 57 (May 1975), pp. 155–63. (See the latter article for a brief review of the literature on empirical analysis of the wealth-age relationship.)

25. Population statistics show that of 11.334 million U.S. males aged 40–49 in 1962, 10.444 million survived until 1972.

firms for both 1962 and 1972 the earlier cross-sectional finding that the older a man is in a given year, the greater his wealth is likely to be. For example, in 1962 the 1 percent cutoff point for males of all ages is $106,000. In all age brackets for men 40 and over, however, the 1 percent points are higher than that.[26] Moreover, the higher the age class that year, the higher net worth is likely to be. For example, the first percentile rises steadily—with only one interruption—from $124,000 to $270,000 between the lowest and highest age classes. The same type of pattern is observed for 1972 when this cutoff point rises fairly steadily from $328,000 to $512,000.[27]

These cross-sectional comparisons within each of the two years separately do not reveal the assumed decumulation phase of the simple life-cycle hypothesis. The more directly relevant intertemporal comparison is also available, however. For all three wealth ranks the cutoff point rose between 1962 and 1972 *within each age class*. It is apparent that the lowest age groups scored the biggest percentage gains in the ten-year interval. For example, those in the 40–49 age class of 1962 were about 2.6 times as wealthy in 1972 when they were 50–59 years old. Relative gains by all males under 40 appear even more pronounced, although (because their wealth was much lower) it was not possible to estimate accurately their 1962 wealth levels below the 0.2 percentile. On the basis of the 0.1 and 0.2 percentiles, the wealth of these males rose from $135,000 to $500,000 and from $82,000 to $313,000, respectively, by the year 1972 when their age was 10–49. In other words, based on changes in these very high wealth ranks, the wealth of this large group of young males was 3.7 to 3.8 times as great in 1972 as in 1962. This amounts to a compound annual rate of growth of 11.4 percent over the ten years, compared with about 10 percent for the next higher age bracket.

The higher age classes beginning with ages 50–54 in 1962 scored progressively lower ten-year gains in net worth, reaching a low ratio of about 1.6 to 1.7 in the 65–69 class. The relatively low ratios for this class suggest that during the ten years in the early stage of their retirement these men added relatively less to their wealth than any of the other age classes. As shown in table 3-1, however, their compounded annual rate of accumulation was still estimated at 4.9 to 5.6 percent between 1962 and 1972. That represents substantial accumulation in money terms. Also

26. Note that this is also true of the other wealth ranks, the 0.5 and 2.0 percentiles.
27. As observed earlier, the cross-sectional wealth-age association appears somewhat weaker in 1972 than in 1962, but it is still clearly present.

shown in table 3-1 are real rates of increase; the 65–69 age group showed a 1.5–2.4 percent compounded annual rate of increase in the value of its real wealth, as deflated by the consumer price index.[28] Thus there is no indication that the slowest rate of accumulation found over the ten years— that of men who started out at age 65–69 in 1962—revealed any dissaving either in money or real terms, as would be expected under the life-cycle hypothesis; in fact their wealth continued to grow quite rapidly in money terms and at about a 2 percent real annual rate.[29]

It should also be added that the relatively low rate of accumulation by the 65–69 group after 1962 was still greater in absolute terms than that found for the entire wealth distribution. For example, the first percentile for the 65–69 cohort gained $176,000 in the next ten years. For the entire distribution the gain was only $96,000. Of course this included the much smaller initial wealth levels among young people, but even the lower age classes in table 3-1 did not gain much more than the 65–69 group in absolute terms.

It seems remarkable that the latter age group, which must have received very little in earnings over the next ten years, continued with a fairly high rate of accumulation to ages 75–79. Obviously these men were not generally making large inter vivos gifts during this period—an indication that conforms to earlier Treasury Department evidence.[30] Presumably the low rate of accumulation for this group, compared with that of younger men, was due to the latter both earning and inheriting more. Earning and intergenerational inheriting have not completely ceased by ages 65–69, but they have undoubtedly tapered off sharply. This raises another remarkable point revealed by table 3-1. Not only were men 75 and over in 1962 wealthier than the 65–69 group; they also achieved a

28. In the 1962–72 interval the consumer price index rose at a 3.3 percent compound annual rate, and the GNP deflator increased at a 3.4 percent rate.

29. Saving is again being interpreted broadly here to include changes in asset value, in either money or real terms. It is possible that a dissaving out of current income occurred but was more than offset by net capital gains and inheritances. It should be added that the indicated increase in the wealth of men in their retirement years may have been due to a statistical bias to be discussed later—a bias caused by wealthy men being likely to live longer. The estimated 1972 percentiles for the original 1962 cohort could be biased upward if the wealthier members of the 1962 group tended to outlast the less wealthy members. This would not mean that the actual share of 1972 survivors in the older age groups is overstated. It would simply mean that the *gain* by these survivors would overstate the gain by the original 1962 cohort.

30. See Joseph A. Pechman, *Federal Tax Policy* (3d ed., Brookings Institution, 1977), pp. 231–32.

considerably higher rate of growth and even achieved rates of accumulation about on a par with the wealth distribution as a whole. These elderly men obviously could have benefited little from earnings or intergenerational transfers in the ten-year interval that took them to age 85 and over. Indeed their accumulation must have derived almost entirely from property income, capital gains, and inheritance from wives. Yet they accumulated wealth more rapidly than the 65–69 group. The younger cohort almost certainly had more earnings and intergenerational transfers. This could have been offset by frequent inheritances by the older men from decedent wives and lower mortality rates among wealthy men.[31]

Although the wealth estimates in table 3-1 for age cohorts over a ten-year interval may seem rather striking, they should be interpreted with caution. Two important qualifications should be mentioned.

First, it is probably most appropriate to stress the estimates presented in real terms at the right of the table. The indicated steady gains in real wealth with age are at substantially lower rates than in terms of current dollars. However, even the 4.8 percent rate of increase—the lowest in the table—still represents a 1.5 percent real rate of growth. A similar analysis by Shorrocks of British data on real wealth (also using the consumer price index as a deflator) showed, as found here, a steady accumulation of wealth through the retirement age and no decumulation phase.[32] Shorrocks found that in real terms the wealth-age profiles usually flatten out at about age 70.

The second qualification, mentioned in note 31, was also analyzed by Shorrocks on the basis of British data.[33] In effect he argued that it was inappropriate to regard survivors among cohorts as a random sample of the original groups being analyzed. The estate multiplier estimates attempt to take account of indicated lower mortality rates among wealthy persons. This same differential should also be allowed for in the cohort analysis because it presumably leads to a higher proportion of wealthy persons in each cohort over time. Adjusting for this, Shorrocks found that the age-wealth profile based on nominal wealth continued to slope upward. When wealth was deflated, however, the slopes were reduced and the profiles tended to peak out at age 65–70 and begin a significant de-

31. The appropriate interpretation of inheritances from wives is not obvious. For example, on a family basis there is no increase in wealth. A potential bias to be discussed later may be especially important here. The greater the age, the greater the selectivity produced by the lower mortality rates among wealthy men.

32. Shorrocks, "The Age-Wealth Relationship," pp. 158–59.

33. Ibid., pp. 155–63.

cline. But this decline was very modest (1 percent) for the highest wealth percentile studied. It should be mentioned that the deflated rates of increase for older persons found for the United States in the present study (table 3-1) were considerably higher than the British results of Shorrocks. This suggests that the mortality adjustment would more or less level out the real wealth-age profiles for older persons shown in table 3-1.

Of course, the absence of a postretirement decumulation phase in the U.S. distributions is not offered as general evidence against even this simple variant of the life-cycle hypothesis discussed here. In the first place, the present evidence pertains only to the top 2 percent of wealthholders. Evidence on lower ranks, if available, might well show the same decline in wealth in later years found by Shorrocks. It may be that dissaving out of income would predominate in lower ranks but is swamped by capital gains and inheritances in the data used here. Moreover, the decumulation phase is only one aspect of the general theoretical construct underlying life-cycle saving models. Indeed the accumulation phase before retirement that also characterizes such models is strongly in evidence in the present findings.

What is the implication of table 3-1 for any attempt to evaluate the role of the wealth-age relationship in generating wealth inequality? First, the pronounced rate of growth of money and real wealth over the working years confirms that lifetime accumulation is clearly one factor perpetuating inequality. The slower rate of growth during retirement years means that age differentials are less responsible for generating inequality than they would be if accumulation had continued at the same pace as before. On the other hand, this finding indicates a stronger role for age than would be the case if wealth were found to decline sharply in the later years.

Finally, the price change and mortality rate qualifications of the cohort analysis can be viewed from an entirely different perspective. They certainly need to be considered if one is trying to track the wealth changes of a given cohort over time—as in any evaluation of the life-cycle hypothesis. But in simply trying to evaluate the role of age differentials in the inequality of wealth in a given year, a cross-sectional analysis may actually be more appropriate. In that case one need not deflate or take account of the lower mortality of the rich. No bias is present in their share, as seen in a cross section. What is called for is a traditional analysis of variance that seeks to determine what fraction of the total variance of wealth (or its logarithm) is accounted for by its variation with age. Such an analysis is hampered, however, by the absence of data about the entire distribution (as well as the substantial frequency of units with negative net worth). A pragmatic substitute for the analysis of variance is adopted in the next section. It entails a comparison of wealth inequality within age groups to the overall inequality of wealth.

Inequality within Homogeneous Age Classes in the United Kingdom and the United States

If the positive wealth-age relation were a very important determinant of inequality, one would expect inequality to be very much less within homogeneous age groups. Indeed under the extreme version of the life-cycle hypothesis—with earnings assumed equal—there would be complete equality among people of the same age. Atkinson again pioneered in demonstrating that inequality within British age groups was not significantly less than overall inequality.[34] The Royal Commission once again followed this up with an assertion of the great importance of allowing for the inequality of earnings.[35]

The preliminary finding of the commission is that the distribution of wealth within age groups is indeed generally similar to the distribution among the entire population. In its opinion, however, this does not necessarily constitute a strong refutation of the life-cycle theory. The argument was that the introduction of inequality of earnings into the life-cycle model makes room for very great inequality among age groups, with such inequality depending on the inequality of earnings. The commission goes even further by claiming that "it is certainly not inconceivable that the distribution of wealth within age groups may be as unequal, and possibly under certain circumstances even more unequal, than in the population as a whole, and yet be consistent with a very strong life-cycle effect."[36]

This extreme case contemplated by the commission seems highly unlikely in the real world. In terms of figure 3-2, for example, one could focus on the peak wealth level at the time of retirement—a level that varies greatly with the degree of lifetime income inequality among persons of that age. Considering only the high-income profile in the figure, it is obvious that the *absolute* inequality at the time of retirement is greater than overall inequality. The usual convention is to measure inequality in relative terms, however. If one accepts the three triangles as depicting

34. Atkinson, "Distribution of Wealth," pp. 246–53.
35. Royal Commission, *Initial Report,* pp. 113–17.
36. Ibid., p. 114.

three earnings-related life cycles, the relative inequality is the same for all ages. For example, the ratio of the wealth of the top-income person to the other two is the same for all ages. The relative inequality measured around the mean for all age classes will inevitably be higher. It is indeed conceivable that the variance within age classes can be greater than over-all despite a strong wealth-age relationship, but it is difficult to rationalize a plausible pattern.[37]

The Royal Commission suggested that a more appropriate test of the life-cycle theory would be an examination of the wealth-age relationship itself. For this purpose it computed, in effect, the ratio of the mean wealth in each age class to overall mean wealth. As in the United States, a strong though inconsistent wealth-age relationship was found. There was a fairly strong positive association in 1954 and 1963–67. For 1972 the relation is much weaker, especially for males.[38] The commission concluded that these findings support the life-cycle theory only to a limited degree. The figures show a positive wealth-age relationship but no evidence of de-cumulation after retirement. It is noted, however, that the inclusion of accrued pension claims, which obviously have a strong traditional life-cycle pattern, might produce the hypothesized wealth-age profile.

Table 3-1 has already shown a positive wealth-age association for the United States on both a cross-sectional basis and with respect to changes over time within given age cohorts. It seems reasonable to concur with the Royal Commission in recognizing that the wealth-age relationship—whatever its shape—plays some part in generating observed inequality. But once again, the mere existence of the relationship is not sufficient to prove its importance. On the other hand, there have been persuasive ef-forts by Atkinson and others to show that various conceivable life-cycle patterns are entirely insufficient to generate the inequality of wealth as we know it. Moreover, the opinion here is that the Royal Commission's case against comparing the inequality of wealth within age groups with overall inequality is not a strong one. It amounts simply to asserting without proof that the great inequality within age classes is due primarily to income dif-ferences, whatever the true wealth-age profile. For this reason this com-

37. Marc Nerlove told me that an analogous variance comparison in a study a generation ago revealed greater variance of the weights of baby armadillos within litters than overall. One or two of the babies in each litter apparently got the lion's share of the milk.

38. As reported earlier, the wealth-age relationship in the United States was also relatively weak in 1972, but the sex difference was in the opposite direction—weaker for females.

parison, first made by Atkinson, will be considered here on the basis of the U.S. data discussed in chapter 2.

Table 2-3 offered a basis for comparing inequality within three major U.S. age classes with overall inequality. Pareto slopes for married men and women were given for the years 1962 and 1972. These Pareto slopes are recapitulated with greater age detail in table 3-2, along with the related mean net worth of persons above the $100,000 net worth level. There is no evidence in this table of any general tendency for wealth to be any less unequal within the three age subgroups than overall.

The greater the Pareto slope, the less the estimated inequality. For five age classes of men in 1962—those between 40 and 70 years of age—inequality was less than the overall figure, but it was greater among younger and older men in the other five age classes. For women in 1962 and both men and women in 1972, inequality within age classes was less than the overall figure in only a minority of the ten age groups. So, not only is the expected greater homogeneity of wealth within age groups nowhere to be seen, but greater inequality within age classes was more frequently observed.

The mean net worth is perhaps a more straightforward inequality measure than the Pareto slope. The greater the mean in this top net worth class, the greater the inequality. For another rough comparison it is interesting to average these means across age classes. For 1962 the averages are $306,000 for men and $339,000 for women—considerably higher in each case than the overall figure.[39] The within-age means for men in 1972 average $273,000, or slightly less than the overall figure, but for women the average for the ten age classes is $291,000—virtually the same as the overall mean. The net import of these various comparisons is to suggest that there is absolutely no evidence of any general tendency toward less inequality within homogeneous age classes—at least not at high wealth levels.[40]

This analysis of top wealthholders with a net worth of over $100,000 provides no evaluation of the overall role of age as a factor in inequality

39. This $339,000 figure for women is perhaps biased upward by the extremely high mean in the small top age class. This could be due to one extremely wealthy person.

40. Similar conclusions were reached by James D. Smith, Stephen D. Franklin, and Douglas A. Wion on the basis of Lorenz curves ("Financial Concentration in the United States," Paper 1208-2 [Urban Institute, 1975; processed]). These Lorenz curves were estimated for the entire wealth distribution on the basis of data for a few percent at the top. Despite the roughness of such extrapolations they appear to confirm the present analysis, which is explicitly confined to net worth levels over $100,000.

The Life-Cycle Hypothesis 69

Table 3-2. Measures of Inequality of Wealth: Pareto Slopes and Mean Net Worth of Married Persons above the $100,000 Level, by Age and Sex, 1962 and 1972
Mean net worth in thousands of dollars

Year and age class	Men		Women	
	Pareto slope[a]	Mean net worth	Pareto slope[a]	Mean net worth
1962				
All ages	1.535	287.0	1.462	316.6
Under 40	1.378	364.3	1.403	348.1
40–49	1.592	268.8	1.487	305.4
50–54	1.597	267.6	1.545	283.4
55–59	1.549	282.3	1.438	328.5
60–64	1.558	279.1	1.400	349.9
65–69	1.573	274.5	1.471	312.3
70–74	1.519	292.5	1.581	272.0
75–79	1.474	311.1	1.457	318.9
80–84	1.414	341.4	1.411	343.2
85 and over	1.357	379.9	1.235	524.9
1972				
All ages	1.528	289.2	1.525	290.6
Under 40	1.612	263.3	1.451	321.7
40–49	1.575	273.9	1.598	267.2
50–54	1.602	266.0	1.491	303.7
55–59	1.504	298.5	1.516	293.9
60–64	1.541	284.9	1.572	274.9
65–69	1.491	303.6	1.467	314.1
70–74	1.464	315.4	1.492	303.1
75–79	1.435	330.0	1.691	244.8
80–84	1.460	317.6	1.515	294.1
85 and over	1.369	370.9	1.520	292.3

Sources: U.S. Internal Revenue Service, *Statistics of Income—1962, Personal Wealth Estimated from Estate Tax Returns* (Government Printing Office, 1967), pp. 48–50; and ibid., *1972*, pp. 43, 45.

a. This slope is negative. Absolute value, *a*, derived from $\overline{NW} = [a(a - 1)]$ ($100,000), where $\overline{NW}$ is mean net worth over $100,000. See R. G. D. Allen, *Mathematical Analysis for Economists* (St. Martin's, 1969), p. 408. The Pareto slopes differ slightly from those reported in table 2-3 because the data used here exclude persons of unknown age.

throughout the distribution. Given data for the entire range, it would be tempting to ask the extent to which variation *across* age groups explains overall inequality. Such data are available from the Federal Reserve survey on the size distribution of family net worth as of December 31, 1962.[41] The frequency of negative wealth and the extreme skewness of the distribution, however, discourage the application of the standard analysis of variance. Instead, a purely descriptive rank analysis is applied in table 3-3.

41. Dorothy S. Projector and Gertrude S. Weiss, *Survey of Financial Characteristics of Consumers* (Board of Governors of the Federal Reserve System, 1966), p. 96.

Table 3-3. Net Worth Medians by Age of Head of Household and Rank in the Overall Net Worth Distribution, December 31, 1962

Age of head of household	Median net worth (thousands of dollars)	Percentile rank of median in overall distribution
Under 35	0.8	25
35–44	6.6	50
45–54	10.5	61
55–64	13.2	65
65 and over	9.7	59
All ages	6.7	50

Source: Derived by linear interpolation in the percentage cumulative frequency distributions, from data in Dorothy S. Projector and Gertrude S. Weiss, *Survey of Financial Characteristics of Consumers* (Board of Governors of the Federal Reserve System, 1966), p. 96.

Rather than analyzing the effect of variations of means by age (unknown), the table records medians by age.

The medians for the poorest age class (under 35) and the wealthiest (55–64) appear to depart substantially enough from the grand median to make a significant contribution to overall inequality. It is also interesting to note that the highest wealth class shows a lower median wealth than the 55–64 age group—the first evidence found here of the decumulation phase suggested by the life-cycle savings models. As surmised earlier, it appears that the wealth-age association may be stronger at lower wealth levels than within the top ranks analyzed here previously, and postretirement dissaving may also be more typical of these low wealth ranks.

The last column of table 3-3 attempts to quantify on a rank basis the importance of the wealth-age profile. The age group medians are restated in terms of their ranks within the overall distribution. Thus it is shown that the median wealth of the young age group falls at the first quartile of the distribution for all age groups—a full quartile below the grand median. The wealthiest age class is at the 65th percentile—appreciably above the grand median. Then the over-65 group shows a decline to the 59th percentile. These differences in rank seem sufficient to indicate a more significant role of the wealth-age profile in the full range of the wealth distribution.

What can be concluded from these tests? The analysis based on the upper tail of the distribution does not explicitly refute the Royal Commission's suggestion that a substantial part of the inequality within age classes *could* be due to saving differentials created by income differentials. Yet it is difficult to accept the other part of the commission's argument—

that a powerful life-cycle pattern could also be present in these high wealth ranks. If the wealth-age relationship were really very strong, it is difficult to explain its failure to cause greater inequality overall than within age groups. The implication of the London *Times* editorial quoted earlier was that a major part of wealth inequality is of a benign form generated by a life cycle of savings. From the U.S. data in table 3-2, as in the British case, it seems reasonable to conclude that this argument, at least, is not supportable on the basis of U.S. data for top wealthholders. The crude analysis in table 3-3 offers a modest qualification of this conclusion. It suggests that the wealth-age profile may be playing a more significant role in creating inequality among moderate and lower wealth classes—at least in the preretirement period.

Tentative Conclusions about the Life Cycle as a Competing Explanation of Wealth Inequality

Atkinson and Oulton have marshalled impressive quasi-empirical illustrations indicating that the traditional wealth-age profile cannot possibly account for a major part of inequality. The Royal Commission essentially agrees but also concurs with the analysis of U.S. data just presented, as well as with some evidence in chapter 2, that independent accumulation over a lifetime may be relatively more important among lower wealth classes.

Table 3-1 confirmed a positive wealth-age association in the United States roughly comparable to that reported by the Royal Commission. Table 3-2 adds impressive evidence that substantial wealth accumulation continues beyond retirement. But neither the U.S. nor the British evidence proves the wealth-age relationship of the life-cycle type or any other to be a major factor in generating inequality. The imputation of accrued pension claims might well move the profile toward the traditional life-cycle shape, as Feldstein has suggested.[42] There is no reason to suppose, however, that this will substantially increase the magnitude of the effect of age on inequality. On the other hand, the wealth-age profile is clearly more important among lower wealth ranks. At the same time, the decumulation phase suggested by the cross-sectional analysis in table 3-3 would make

42. Feldstein, "Social Security and the Distribution of Wealth," pp. 800, 806.

for a lower degree of age-generated inequality than if accumulation continued rapidly beyond retirement.[43]

Finally, the opinion here is that the most important evidence against the
wealth-age relationship as a major factor among top wealthholders is the
inequality within age groups. For both the United States and the United
Kingdom it was found to be about the same as overall inequality. One
can only reject this negative indication if one is willing to assume that a
major reason for inequality within age groups is saving differentials caused
by the inequality of incomes. There is no solid evidence that routine saving out of earnings has much to do with the generation of large fortunes.
The Royal Commission's analysis of income differentials showed a weak
effect among the top 1 percent—most of whom do not have really great
wealth. It seems more likely that the larger fortunes among these are built
primarily out of extraordinary rates of return and capital gains on rare
and highly successful ventures, plus intergenerational transfers. While
extraordinary gain and intergenerational transfers are difficult to separate,
both are probably more important than routine life-cycle saving in generating the large shares of the top wealth ranks.

43. The relationships in table 3-3 require qualification, however. The data are on
a household basis, unlike the previously presented evidence on individuals. Since
households with heads over 65 are relatively small, their wealth would be higher on a
per capita basis.

chapter four **Intergenerational Wealth Relationships:**
A Broader View

The intergenerational transmission of economic status takes place in unmeasurable and even unobservable ways. A son is apt to achieve an income and occupational status that is fairly strongly correlated with that of his father. The media through which economic status is transmitted across generations vary from a subtle "rubbing off" of opportunity (or the lack of it) to the explicit provision of educational opportunity and direct and explicit material gifts or bequests. The last of these has been the subject of this analysis. Now it is appropriate to give some consideration to the overall relationship of the material wealth of fathers and sons—including that aspect of this relationship that exists independently of explicit gifts or bequests.[1] This, of course, is a broader version of the inheritance concept than that embodied in explicit material transfers. It embraces all causes of the intergenerational association of the wealth of fathers and sons—known and unknown—of which gifts and bequests are only one component.

Although the interpretation of the gross intergenerational wealth association is not straightforward, it is a valuable supplement to the kind of research previously discussed. Indeed the British research in this area is a major empirical contribution to the evaluation of the effects of the

1. The emphasis on the *male* intergenerational relationship in studies to date was pragmatic. Parents of married women were difficult to trace, since the death certificates of these women did not include their maiden names. In any case women have had little opportunity to accumulate wealth independently. Since the objective of such studies is to distinguish the effects of intergenerational transfers from those of independent accumulation, the father-son wealth relationship is more revealing. But it should be recognized that this focus excludes the tendency of sons and daughters of wealthy people to marry each other—a tendency that is a major factor in the perpetuation of inequality.

father-son wealth relationship on the distribution of wealth. Since no such research on material wealth has been completed in this country, the best that can be done is to ask if any inferences concerning the United States can be drawn from the unique British analysis of experience over the last half century.

Focus of the British Studies

The primary objective of intergenerational analysis is to evaluate the impact of inheritance on the relative lifetime economic status of individuals and families. It is important, then, to consider first just what relationships have been uncovered by the kind of studies to be discussed. These studies focus on the relationship between the *material* wealth of persons of one generation and the wealth of their descendants. It should be remembered, however, that human wealth (exemplified by education and earning power) is generally playing an undercover role. Studies of the association between the material wealth of father and son have offered important insights in the past, but some interpretations of the findings may have been misleading. There has been a tendency to view the association of the material wealth of father and son as a measure of the importance of material inheritance as a factor making for inequality. Clearly this type of inheritance is not the only factor reflected in such an association.

Viewing paternal wealth as an explanatory variable, it is apparent that the impact of this wealth is transmitted to sons via environmental advantage, education provided, and other channels—not via financial transfers alone. In any such statistical relationship the father's wealth will tend to proxy for all advantages or disadvantages associated with inherited position.[2] Although the components cannot be broken down by this form of analysis, the father-son wealth relationship is useful as an overall indication of the head start or handicap that can be attributed to family background. So the total impact of all factors associated with a father's wealth deserves consideration.

The pioneering effort by Wedgwood relating the probated wills of a sample of sons to the wills of their fathers was followed up by a similar important study reported in 1962 by Harbury.[3] The latter undertook an

2. This includes inherited wealth-making ability, if that is a hereditary characteristic.
3. Josiah Wedgwood, *The Economics of Inheritance* (London: Routledge, 1929;

extremely careful search for the name and date of death of the fathers of wealthy men who died in 1956–57. Harbury ended up with 618, or 95 percent, of the fathers' wills identified beyond reasonable doubt. He portrayed the father-son wealth association by displaying the wealth distribution of fathers of a given group of wealthy sons. The bulk of his sample consisted of all 391 men who died in 1956–57 with estates in the £100,000–£200,000 class. His figures imply that the probability is 67 percent that the father of a randomly chosen man in this wealthy 1956–57 group left over £10,000. This was a very large sum a generation earlier, and it is clear that most of the fathers of Harbury's wealthy sample were themselves wealthy.

Harbury's findings were summed up in an empirical relationship illustrated in figure 4-1. The empirically derived curve shows the percentage of wealthy sons whose fathers left estates greater than amounts plotted on the horizontal axis. For example, 72 percent of fathers of sons in the top (£100,000–£200,000) wealth class had estates greater than £5,000. The "hypothetical" curve represents what the corresponding percentage would have been without any father-son wealth association; it is simply the cumulative wealth distribution of *all* fathers of sons who died in 1956–57. The curve would obviously lie close to the two axes; for example, one can safely infer that less than 1 percent of these fathers left estates of £5,000 or more. The gap between the two curves is best seen as illustrating a definite relationship between the wealth of fathers and sons.[4] Harbury goes further and interprets the departure of the empirical curve from the hypothetical as "broadly speaking [a measure of] the importance of inheritance in the compiling of personal fortunes."[5] This is implausible if the reference is to *material* inheritance alone; however, the analysis is perhaps adequate for his objective of comparing the impact of inheritance in the twenties and fifties.[6] Even so, as

---

Kennikatt, 1971), chap. 6; and C. D. Harbury, "Inheritance and the Distribution of Personal Wealth in Britain," *Economic Journal*, vol. 72 (December 1962), pp. 845–68.

4. The empirical curve measures a conditional probability; for example, given that a son left £100,000–£200,000, the probability that his father left more than £5,000 is 72 percent. The hypothetical curve specifies no condition; for example, for a randomly chosen son dying in the same period, the probability that his father left more than £5,000 is less than 1 percent (as will be shown later).

5. Harbury, "Inheritance and the Distribution of Personal Wealth in Britain," p. 854.

6. Harbury's work does not, of course, separate the roles of material inheritance from that of inherited environment or ability and drive. The fact that the great wealth

Figure 4-1. Probability That a Member of the Top Wealth Class Was the Son of a Father Whose Estate Exceeded Any Given Amount[a]

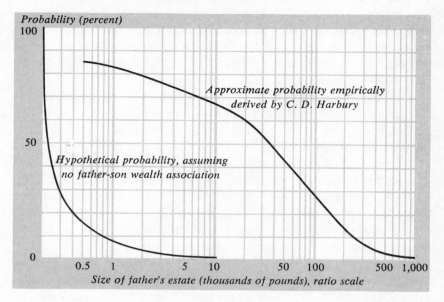

Probability (percent)

Approximate probability empirically derived by C. D. Harbury

Hypothetical probability, assuming no father-son wealth association

Size of father's estate (thousands of pounds), ratio scale

[a] The top wealth class comprises decedents leaving estates valued between £100,000 and £200,000.

in the case of the Lorenz curve or Pareto line, the interpretation of the curve is ambiguous. For example, it provides no measure of the *degree* of impact of inheritance. For this reason a regression analysis of the father-son wealth relationship seems appropriate. A preliminary version will be offered after a brief summary of the implications of the Wedgwood and Harbury findings.

The Findings of Wedgwood and Harbury

Chapter 2 presented estimates suggesting a strong quantitative role of intergenerational transfers in the creation of wealth. Chapter 3 was largely an effort to show that routine saving, as under the life-cycle hypothesis, falls far short of explaining the inequality of wealth. Even if the latter

---

of fathers "explains" the great wealth of sons does not imply that material inheritance is the key factor. As indicated earlier, the father's wealth is also proxying for the advantage of simply being part of the wealthy family.

conclusion is accepted, however, the importance of inheritance as an alternative explanation is not thereby established. As discussed in chapter 1, it is clear that many great fortunes are amassed quickly within a single generation. The Wedgwood-Harbury type of analysis cannot directly weigh the relative importance of the different avenues to wealth. But an assessment of the overall intergenerational association makes an important contribution to the question.

As will be shown in the following section, Wedgwood's findings for 1924–26 were confirmed to a remarkable degree a generation later by Harbury's data for 1956–57.[7] Since the intergenerational relationships in those two periods were so nearly the same, it is convenient to focus here on the work of Harbury and associates.[8]

This work is summed up in table 4-1, which measures all wealth levels in 1956–57 prices.[9] The major impact of the table is best seen in the largest samples—those for sons with estates of £100,000 and over in constant prices. These are estimated conditional distributions of the size of the father's estate, given that the son's estate was in this bracket. For example, the percentage of fathers who also left estates of £100,000 and over were 51, 45, and 35 in 1956–57, 1965, and 1973, respectively. The first two percentages are remarkably high, especially when it is recognized that the £100,000 real wealth level of fathers generally meant a wealth *rank* even higher than that of their sons.[10] If one guesses that a £50,000 real wealth level for a father was more comparable in rank to the £100,000 level for the son, table 4-1 suggests that 57–58 percent of the

7. The comparison in the next section of the Harbury and Wedgwood results utilizes current (rather than real) values of the wealth of fathers and sons. This poses no serious problem, since the logarithmic transformation used there yields an answer that is fairly impervious to the deflation of fathers' and sons' wealth. (The elasticity estimates are not completely unaffected by deflation, because the dates of death of the fathers vary; however, these dates have a relatively small variance.) For some purposes the constant price evaluations used in Harbury's later work and to be discussed here are more appropriate.

8. Three papers in the *Economic Journal* cover three successive intergenerational studies: Harbury, "Inheritance and the Distribution of Personal Wealth in Britain"; C. D. Harbury and P. C. McMahon, "Inheritance and the Characteristics of Top Wealth Leavers in Britain," vol. 83 (September 1973), pp. 810–33; and C. D. Harbury and D. M. W. M. Hitchens, "The Inheritances of Top Wealth Leavers: Some Further Evidence," vol. 86 (June 1976), pp. 321–26.

9. In the absence of appropriate asset price indexes, consumer price indexes were used for deflation.

10. Absolute real wealth levels were substantially lower in the earlier periods when most fathers died.

Table 4-1. Relation of Estates of Fathers and Sons, Valued at Constant 1956–57 Average Prices, 1956–57, 1965, and 1973
Cumulative percentages

Size of son's estate (thousands of pounds)	Period[a]	Size of father's estate (pounds)										Number in sample
		Over 1,000,000	Over 500,000	Over 250,000	Over 100,000	Over 50,000	Over 25,000	Over 10,000	Over 5,000	Over 1,000	Less than 1,000	
500 and over	1956–57	35	42	46	62	77	77	81	81	85	100	26
	1965	17	17	50	50	50	50	50	50	67	100	6
	1973	25	25	50	63	63	63	88	88	88	100	8
300–500	1956–57	22	32	46	56	63	66	68	71	83	100	41
	1965	14	43	57	57	100	100	100	100	100	100	7
	1973	17	33	33	67	83	83	83	83	83	100	6
200–300	1956–57	12	23	35	55	66	68	73	81	85	100	72
	1965	0	18	46	73	91	100	100	100	100	100	11
	1973	11	22	22	44	61	72	78	89	89	100	18
100–200	1956–57	5	15	29	48	59	67	75	78	85	100	391
	1965	3	7	18	38	49	60	74	79	82	100	68
	1973	3	7	15[b]	27[b]	41[b]	51[b]	66	68	76	100	74
100 and over	1956–57	9	19	33	51	57	68	75	78	85	100	530
	1965	4	12	26	45	58	67	77	82	85	100	92
	1973	7	12	20[b]	35[b]	48	58[b]	71	74	79	100	106
All sons (all estate sizes)	1956–57	n.a.	n.a.	n.a.	0.11	0.26	0.56	1.26	2.30	6.85	100	n.a.
	1965	n.a.	n.a.	n.a.	0.13	0.32	0.74	1.90	3.50	10.33	100	n.a.
	1973	n.a.	n.a.	n.a.	0.14	0.35	0.83	2.23	4.09	12.32	100	n.a.

Source: C. D. Harbury and D. M. W. M. Hitchens, "The Inheritances of Top Wealth Leavers: Some Further Evidence," *Economic Journal*, vol. 86 (June 1976), pp. 324–25.
a. 1956–57 = average for the two years.
b. Statistically significant differences between 1973 and 1956–57 at the 5 percent level.
n.a. = not available.

wealthy decedents in the first two periods had fathers whose estates fell in the same top rank.[11] Less than one-half of the sons descended from fathers who left estates under £ 50,000. These data offer persuasive evidence that in Britain, in those days at least, the nouveau riche were a minority.

This strong intergenerational wealth association does not, of course, prove that the majority of sons were wealthy only because of material transfers. Other advantages also accrued to sons of the wealthy. Moreover, the sons could have achieved extraordinary independent accumulation or exceptionally high rates of return on small inheritances. Nevertheless, the fact that nearly 60 percent of the sons had fathers who were in the same high rank as they were is a powerful indication that wealth-building is strongly aided by an advantaged start in life.

While most wealthy men descended from wealthy fathers, an appreciable minority of these sons may have been nouveau riche. Indeed 15 to 21 percent had fathers who left estates of £ 1,000 or less in 1956–57 prices. Of course, these fathers were not necessarily poor during their lifetimes. Some were undoubtedly examples of that minority of individuals who actually draw down their savings, in keeping with the life-cycle hypothesis discussed in chapter 3. Moreover, even a mere £ 1,000 estate was sufficient to place a father among the top 7 to 12 percent of decedent males of his time.[12] It also is likely that some of these sons had wealthy mothers or other relatives. Even so, it is important to note that there is a significant minority of these wealthy sons whose fathers were not wealthy at death. Although only a small minority of the sons could have been nouveau riche, it is these cases that attract attention and lend credence to the conception of substantial vertical mobility in industrial societies. What is shown in table 4-1 is only the tip of the iceberg. What happened to the other sons of men with estates under £ 1,000?

The fact that some wealthy persons emerge from disadvantaged beginnings cannot be put into a realistic perspective on the basis of the data on wealthy sons appearing in table 4-1. Each line representing wealthy sons in that table is typified by the top curve in figure 4-1. The table reports the percentage of fathers of wealthy sons with estates above each specified level. However, it is useful to compare these percentages with

11. The assumption that £ 50,000 for fathers is about equivalent in rank to £ 100,000 for sons would be valid if, for example, the fathers were 30 years older and per capita real wealth grew at a 2.3 percent annual rate.

12. See the bottom section of table 4-1.

the wealth distributions of fathers of decedent sons in the general population. Harbury and Hitchens have estimated "the probability of drawing at random a father's estate of more than a given size for each of the sample years."[13] These estimated probabilities have been entered in the bottom section of table 4-1 and interpreted as representing "all sons (all estate sizes)" in the three periods.[14] Each of these lines is typified by the lower curve in figure 4-1 that represents the hypothetical distribution of fathers' wealth on the assumption of independence between a father's wealth and a son's wealth. In other words, for example, although 51 percent of the sons in 1956–57 leaving over £100,000 had fathers with estates above that level, only 0.11 percent of all decedent sons had fathers who were that wealthy. That is, the chance that the father of one of these wealthy sons was similarly wealthy was nearly 500 times the chance that this would be true of the father of a randomly chosen decedent son. This contrast is perhaps unsurpassed in published research as an indicator of the effects of the intergenerational wealth link.

It is interesting to return at this point to the sons whose fathers were not wealthy. In 1956–57, 15 percent of the fathers of sons in the £100,000 class left no more than £1,000. Among the general population of decedent sons, the estimate of such nonwealthy fathers was about 93 percent. This contrast seems far less striking than in the previously described case of wealthy fathers. But such a comparison may be misleading. The chance that the randomly chosen son has a very wealthy father is remote. Estimates were not even provided for fathers' estate sizes over £250,000. Yet among all categories of wealthy sons in table 4-1 a substantial fraction had fathers of comparable wealth. For example, 11 fathers of 26 sons with estates of £500,000 and over left that much themselves. So the higher the wealth level of fathers and sons being considered, the greater the contrast between the probability that a wealthy son will have such a wealthy father and the remote probability in the case of a randomly chosen son. At the same time, it should be noted that among the four classes of wealthy sons there was no appreciable difference in the frequency with which they descended from "poor" fathers.

Table 4-1 does not provide explicit measurement of the father-son wealth correlation, but the positive association is fairly clear. The sam-

---

13. Harbury and Hitchens, "The Inheritances of Top Wealth Leavers," p. 325.
14. On the basis of the description given by Harbury and Hitchens, this probability has been interpreted in table 4-1 as the estimated percentage of the fathers of all decedent sons in a given year whose wealth was above the specified level.

ples for the higher wealth levels of sons are very small, except for 1956–57. The father-son wealth correlations appear somewhat irregular even then—another reason for the correlation-regression analysis suggested in the next section. It should also be noted that the depicted range of sons' wealth is not very great relatively—except for the open-ended class at the top. Even so, the number of fathers with estates over £100,000, for example, progresses fairly steadily from 48 percent in the lowest of the sons' wealth ranks to 62 percent at the top. More striking is the variation in the number of sons who had the wealthiest fathers—millionaires (at 1956–57 prices) at death. Only 5 percent of the fathers of the "poorest" sons left estates of this size, but 35 percent of the fathers of the wealthiest sons were in that category.[15]

It is not easy to interpret these figures as direct evidence of the influence of fathers' wealth on sons' wealth. The studies were conducted in the reverse direction. They took the wealth of the sons as the starting point and measured the wealth of their fathers.[16] But the small (5 percent) incidence of millionaires among fathers of the least wealthy sons suggests that the sons of very wealthy men are unlikely to have wealth as low as £100,000–£200,000. On the other hand, the 35 percent estimate indicates that very wealthy men are likely to have sons of comparable wealth.

The data of Harbury and associates show some indirect evidence of a significant decline in the role of fathers' wealth in generating the fortunes of sons. By 1973 the percentage of sons with estates over £100,000 whose fathers left that much or more had declined to 35—compared with 51 percent half a generation earlier.[17] This suggests that estate taxes may have had a substantially greater impact on the estates of fathers of the 1973 decedents than was true earlier. On the other hand, Harbury and Hitchens note that a higher proportion of the fathers in the 1973 sample died during the Great Depression. This could have depressed the measured wealth of these fathers in a way not adequately allowed for by the deflation procedure used in their study. That is, the deflated estate size of these fathers may represent a higher wealth *rank* than the same wealth level before or after the depression. While this qualification cannot be

15. The 35 percent figure is based on a sample of only 26 fathers, but the smoothness of the progression (5, 12, 22, 35) makes it plausible.

16. This problem is considered in the regression analysis in the next section.

17. These comparisons would be more meaningful if based on ranks instead of absolute wealth levels.

evaluated quantitatively, the trend and the magnitude of the drop in the number of wealthy fathers appears sharp enough to indicate that estate tax policy may have appreciably weakened the father-son wealth link and helped reduce wealth inequality.[18]

Regression Analysis of the Wedgwood and Harbury Data

The relationships illustrated in figure 4-1 and reported in detail in table 4-1 are highly revealing, but there is no way of giving a capsule summary of their structure and the degree of association. It seems appropriate to try to go beyond the Wedgwood-Harbury descriptive format and ask whether the father-son wealth relationship can be further clarified by conventional regression and correlation analysis. What follows is a preliminary effort along these lines. It is limited to the 1924–26 Wedgwood data and the largest Harbury sample (1956–57 decedent sons).

Harbury has indicated that he refrained from an extensive statistical evaluation of the results because of a lack of confidence in the individual wealth estimates in an age of tax avoidance. It may be presumed, however, that this "errors-in-variables" reality is most likely to bias the regression slope downward. In any case even the most primitive analysis may be of interest.[19] This father-son information is the most relevant now available, and an exploratory evaluation of the impact of parental wealth is essential for the ultimate decision on whether the relationships are important enough to deserve detailed study.

Harbury and Wedgwood present bivariate percentage frequency distributions that make possible a two-variable regression analysis.[20] But the

18. It is interesting to find that the indicated decline in the frequency of wealthy fathers is somewhat greater and more consistent for the £100,000–£200,000 class of son's estate than for wealthier sons. It is also more consistently significant even though the sample size is smaller. This appears to weigh against the hypothesis and finding of chapter 2 that the role of intergenerational transfers is greater the higher the wealth level. In the British case the rise in estate tax rates may have had less effect on the fathers of very wealthy sons.

19. The regression analysis reported here is a revised version of material reported in an earlier paper: John A. Brittain, "Research on the Transmission of Material Wealth," *American Economic Review*, vol. 63 (May 1973, *Papers and Proceedings, 1972*), pp. 335–45.

20. Since the frequencies were not given by Harbury, the percentage frequencies were applied to the sample size to estimate the frequency in each cell. These were used to weight the point representing the cells. Each point was taken to be the mean in each class estimated roughly on the basis of official death duty statistics.

way in which the samples were chosen produced a methodological difficulty. All of them started with a sample of very wealthy sons and searched for their fathers. It was thus inappropriate to regress sons' wealth on fathers' wealth. The slope of such a regression would overstate the slope of the son-father relationship, as the sons included were restricted to the high wealth range. Since sons' wealth was the predetermined variable in each study, there was no escape from the conceptually awkward decision to treat sons' wealth as the explanatory variable. The logarithmic transformation of each variable was clearly called for to attain approximate normality and constant variance.[21] The father and son variables are measured in thousands of pounds; after transformation to common logarithms they are labeled F and S. The regression equations based on the Harbury (1956–57) and Wedgwood (1924–26) studies are given in equations 5 and 6, respectively (with routine estimates of the standard errors in parentheses):

$$(5) \qquad F = -0.060 + 0.608 \, S$$
$$ (0.388) \quad (0.176)$$

$r^2 = 0.019$; standard error $= 1.01$;

$$(6) \qquad F = -0.007 + 0.609 \, S$$
$$ (0.287) \quad (0.136)$$

$r^2 = 0.107$; standard error $= 1.04$.

The regression slopes appear highly significant, differing from zero by about four standard errors in each case although the statistical significance of the findings is probably exaggerated.[22] In any case point estimates of

21. On a priori grounds the wealth distributions were expected to be, and proved to be, lognormal in this wealth range. Under the transformation the slopes of the father-son regressions are elasticity estimates, and this is an appropriate method for relating these distributions that have greatly different means. The transformation also avoided the need to deflate the wealth data. (It reduces the effect of deflation on the elasticity estimates.)

22. In correspondence and discussions with me, S. J. Prais has argued that the standard errors of the slopes in equations 5 and 6 are biased downward substantially owing to failure to allow for the effect of grouping the data. His estimates of the standard errors in the two equations are 0.72 and 0.25, respectively. However, comparable regressions by Prais using ungrouped observations from other father-son wealth relationships led to significant slopes with standard errors of the same order of magnitude as those given in equations 5 and 6. In any case, since the slopes are not markedly affected by the use of grouped data, the essence of the discussion presented here is not really affected. For an earlier discussion of this methodological problem, see S. J. Prais and J. Aitchison, "The Grouping of Observations in Regression Analysis," *Review of the International Statistical Institute*, vol. 1 (1954), pp. 1–22.

the elasticity and standard error of estimate for the two widely differing time periods agree remarkably.

The stability of these structural estimates over a generation inspires more confidence in the two relationships than could be accorded either alone. The strength of the intergenerational link may be illustrated by applying equation 5 to the case of a man who left £100,000 in 1956–57. The point estimate of his father's estate is £14,300. Assuming normality, the probability is about two-thirds that any such father left between £1,400 and £147,000 (and 0.84 that he left more than £1,400). Although this is a large spread, it covers only relatively wealthy men during that earlier generation; according to one guess, only about 4 percent of the fathers of all 1956–57 decedents left more than the lower limit of £1,400.[23]

The r^2 value under 2 percent found in equation 5 is probably one of the lowest ever published. But it offers a perfect illustration of the frequently misleading nature of the r^2 criterion. The range of the predetermined variable (the wealth of Harbury's very wealthy 1956–57 decedents) was so small that it had no chance to explain a large fraction of the variance. By the identity relating the correlation coefficient, the regression coefficient, and the standard deviations,

$$(7) \qquad\qquad r_{FS} = b_{FS} s_S / s_F.$$

The problem is that in Harbury's sample of very wealthy sons, s_S was restricted to about 0.23, while fathers' wealth ranged widely, producing an s_F of 1.03, leading to an r_{FS} of only 0.14 (and an r^2 of 0.019).

What correlation might be found if the entire range of the bivariate distribution could be studied? One guess can be derived from the official estate distributions covering the top 5 or 10 percent of all individuals dying in 1956–57 and in 1916—the median year of death of the Harbury fathers. The lognormal probability plots of these distributions exhibited such remarkable linearity that extrapolation down to the mean and estimation of standard deviations seemed justified.[24] From these fitted estate distributions emerged estimates of $s_F = 1.23$ and $s_S = 0.83$, indicating a

23. The estimate of 4 percent is based on the official estate-duty statistics for 1916, which Harbury reports as the median year of death of all fathers in the sample. (It was necessary to assume that the estate distribution for the fathers of all men dying in 1956–57 was the same as the 1916 estate distribution.) This 4 percent estimate seems in tune with the 7 percent estimate of the number of fathers' estates over £1,000 (see table 4-1).

24. The cumulative percentage frequency distribution of wealth was transformed to normal deviates that could be used in a linear regression on the logarithm of

substantial decline in the relative inequality of the distribution of estates over this interval. Assuming linearity in the bivariate model, these extrapolations and the Harbury data can be used to manufacture an alternative father-son regression slope estimate of 1.19.[25] Applying equation 6 yields a highly speculative estimate of the overall correlation coefficient at 0.80. Though its credentials are rather forlorn, this estimate at least suggests that the observed correlation coefficient of 0.14 for the truncated Harbury distribution is seriously misleading as evidence of the overall father-son relationship. In this case the twice-observed elasticity of 0.61 is obviously a clearer indication of the intergenerational wealth link. The slope of the regression line seems more important than the substantial variability around it. If valid here, it implies that if A's estate ends up ten times B's, the best estimate is that A's father left four times as much as B's father.

Placing an interpretation on the father-son wealth elasticity found here would require extensive investigation. But a hint is offered by the simple genetic associations observed in the past. Any father-son analysis recalls Galton's classical "law of universal regression." For example, the sons of very tall fathers do not, on the average, inherit the full height of their fathers and are generally shorter, although above the mean. He also found this "regression toward the mean" to be very pronounced, with child-parent regression slopes only about 0.3 for many characteristics from human heights to the size of sweet pea seeds.[26] This is considerably lower than those suggested by the wealth relationships discussed here.

The comparison above tempts one to make the highly speculative observation that the much smaller "regression to the mean" in the case of the wealth variate than in the case of genetic characteristics may offer a crude measure of the special advantage associated with parental wealth over and above that conferred by innate wealth-making ability. This

---

wealth; the result was an r^2 of 0.999 and 1.000 in the two periods and no appreciable departure from linearity. The fitted range of normal deviates was about 1.5–2.0 in width, and it was necessary to extrapolate downward about 1.6 deviates in each case in order to estimate the mean.

25. This was obtained from the line connecting the point representing the overall 1916 and 1956–57 means (through which the regression line must pass) and the corresponding point for Harbury's high-wealth distribution. It should be noted, however, that there is some evidence of convexity downward in the Harbury father-son relationship, although the coefficients on a square term added to equations 5 and 6 were not significant.

26. Francis Galton, "Family Likeness in Stature," in *Proceedings of the Royal Society of London,* vol. 40 (London: Harrison, 1886), p. 55.

proposition, as Blinder has pointed out, is akin to that of Pigou, who suggested that the skewness of income distributions in contrast to the presumed symmetrical distribution of traits such as IQ may reflect inherited material advantage.[27] No claim is made here for either proposition, but both merit consideration. If data were available, it would be more promising to compare in a multivariate model the roles of estimated genetic characteristics such as IQ with environmental or opportunity factors in wealth determination.

Tentative Conclusions from the British Studies and Tentative U.S. Findings

Can any inferences concerning the United States be drawn from the British studies? There has been no solid evidence showing that the intergenerational wealth link is tighter in Britain than in the United States. The conventional view is that class lines are tighter and intergenerational mobility less in Britain. This must be borne in mind in any attempt to "transfer" the British findings to this country.

A comparison of the distribution of wealth in the two countries may offer one clue about the comparative strength of the intergenerational wealth association. Other things being equal, the stronger the influence of inheritance, the greater the inequality of wealth. If indeed the intergenerational association is stronger in Britain, this should be reflected in a greater inequality of wealth.[28] There is some evidence of greater wealth inequality in Britain than in the United States over the years. For example, using similar estate multiplier estimates, Smith and Franklin found a 21 percent share of net worth for the top 1 percent of U.S. adults over 21 in 1972; a roughly comparable British estimate shows a 28 percent share of personal wealth for the top 1 percent of the population over 18.[29] A similar contrast was found in the fifties by Lydall and Lansing on the

---

27. A. C. Pigou, *The Economics of Welfare* (2d ed., London: Macmillan, 1924), cited in Alan S. Blinder, "A Model of Inherited Wealth," *Quarterly Journal of Economics,* vol. 87 (November 1973), pp. 608–09.

28. The ceteris paribus qualification of this reasoning should be emphasized. For example, inheritance could have a stronger effect in Britain only to have this differential offset by greater redistribution of wealth through fiscal policy.

29. Royal Commission on the Distribution of Income and Wealth, *Initial Report on the Standing Reference,* Report 1, Cmnd. 6171 (London: Her Majesty's Stationery Office, 1975), p. 80; and James D. Smith and Stephen D. Franklin, estimates reported in U.S. Bureau of the Census, *Statistical Abstract of the United States, 1975* (Government Printing Office, 1975), p. 410.

basis of survey data.[30] Both of these comparisons suggest that the effect of intergenerational transfers is probably appreciably stronger in Britain, especially when this effect may also be offset more strongly by fiscal redistribution in that country than in the United States. On the other hand, the British studies seem consistent with the speculative finding in chapter 2 of a strong weight of inherited wealth among top U.S. wealthholders.

It is true, of course, that the British studies are unique and not really directly comparable to any of the more fragmentary evidence on the effects of inheritance in this country. For example, the Wedgwood-Harbury type of association is an overall intergenerational wealth link reflecting other influences than gifts and bequests alone. Moreover, the potential inherited wealth of a son generally is only one part of the father's wealth at death—wealth that may be widely distributed among heirs. Despite these qualifications, the indicated strength of the British intergenerational link described in table 4-1 and summarized here in regression relations 5 and 6 is highly impressive. The evidence is perhaps best summed up by those regressions. Although the studies were a generation apart, they agree remarkably on the regression relationship between the wealth of fathers and sons. For any given differential between the wealth of two decedent sons, the twice-obtained 0.61 elasticity offers a reliable "prediction" of the differential between their fathers. For example, consider a moderately wealthy decedent married man 1 percent from the top of the U.S. net worth distribution. Table 2-4 puts his wealth at $399,000 in 1972. Compare him with a poor man who left an estate one-hundredth that size—about $4,000.[31] If the 0.61 coefficient were also valid for the United States today, the best prediction is that the rich man's father left an estate more than 16 times that of the poor man's father. Perfect intergenerational association would yield a prediction of a 100-to-1 ratio for fathers also, but an estimated 16-to-1 ratio is still a remarkable differential.

Preliminary unpublished reports of the first study of the U.S. father-son wealth relationship being conducted by Paul L. Menchik at the Institute for Research on Poverty at the University of Wisconsin show the

30. Harold Lydall and John B. Lansing, "A Comparison of the Distribution of Personal Income and Wealth in the United States and Great Britain," *American Economic Review*, vol. 49 (March 1959), pp. 43–67.

31. Actually a $4,000 estate is not extraordinarily low. A sample of male and female decedents in the Cleveland metropolitan area in 1964–65 showed that 18 percent left less than $2,000. See Marvin B. Sussman, Judith N. Cates, and David T. Smith, *The Family and Inheritance* (Russell Sage Foundation, 1970).

relationship to be at least as strong in the United States as in the British data presented earlier in this chapter.[32] This study reverses the British approach and proceeds from parent to child. Menchik started with a sample of 1,050 Connecticut residents who died in the thirties and forties leaving estates of $40,000 or more. He has since located the estates of 300 of their children who also died in Connecticut and has processed 180 of these.[33] In his regression analysis he sought to control for both the length of time children held their inherited wealth and their age. In the regression equations including wealth and other variables, he found that elasticities of children's wealth with respect to parents' wealth ranged from 0.73 to 0.86. These are even higher than the results reported above for the two-variable analyses of the British data.[34] This preliminary U.S. finding is consistent with the British evidence of limited intergenerational mobility from one wealth class to another.[35]

In sum, the British evidence and preliminary U.S. findings on father-son relationships concur with chapters 2 and 3 in attributing a strong role to inheritance in perpetuating wealth inequality. It also seems appropriate to contrast inheritance—an unearned reward—with earned incomes as targets of redistributive tax policy. If society prefers to apply relatively high rates to unearned rewards, more effective taxation of intergenerational transfers is an appropriate and efficient route toward reduced inequality of wealth. Since unearned rewards have no significant effect on work incentives, it also seems likely that a redistributive policy based on such taxation would have no serious effects on productive efficiency.

32. See Paul L. Menchik, "Intergenerational Transmission of Inequality: An Empirical Study of Wealth Mobility—Some Preliminary Results" (paper presented at the annual meeting of the Midwest Economics Association, St. Louis, Mo., 1977; processed).

33. Menchik discusses the potential bias in these data that include "stayers" only and surmises it to be minor. For an analogous conclusion, see John A. Brittain, *The Inheritance of Economic Status* (Brookings Institution, 1977), pp. 68–69.

34. Menchik has also acquired data on the amount bequeathed to each child. Certain assumptions about the rate of return on inherited wealth enable him to estimate the importance of inheritance in the distribution of wealth. He can also measure the effect of federal and state death taxes. See "The Effect of Material Inheritance, and Inheritance Taxation, on the Distribution of Wealth," *American Economic Review*, vol. 68 (May 1978, *Papers and Proceedings, 1977*, forthcoming).

35. Some problems and possibilities of further father-son wealth analysis in the United States are discussed in the appendix.

appendix **Prospects for Further Research**

This monograph has reviewed some earlier work of British scholars concerning the effects of intergenerational transfers on wealth inequality.[1] Several additional sets of U.S. empirical evidence have been presented, along with a statistical analysis of the British father-son data. It may be useful to set down several lines along which the intergenerational analysis can be pressed further.

Generalizing the Harbury-Wedgwood Approach

A more general analysis of the meaning and importance of the intergenerational link is clearly called for. A more modern version of the concept of regression-to-the-mean should be applied to the father-son data. An example of this kind of application is that of the Markov process in the work of Lee Soltow on Norwegian towns.[2] "Transition matrices" were used to analyze the effect of intergenerational mobility between income classes on the inequality of income over time. The technique provides estimates of interclass mobility and the amount of mobility needed to yield more or less inequality over time. For example, the greater the interclass mobility and the less the initial interclass differentials, the greater the likelihood that inequality will decrease over time. This type of analysis would also be appropriate for application to British and U.S. father-son wealth data.

1. Not yet available is a major new work: A. B. Atkinson and A. J. Harrison, *The Distribution of Personal Wealth in Britain* (Cambridge University Press, forthcoming).
2. See Lee Soltow, *Toward Income Equality in Norway* (University of Wisconsin Press, 1965).

The restriction of the analysis to father-son relationships seems un-necessarily confining. In the first place, nothing has been learned about the role of women in the process of the transmission of wealth from one generation to the next or about the importance of in-laws' wealth. The marital selection process may be especially significant. The tendency for sons of wealthy men to marry daughters of wealthy men should be in-corporated into the model. The logical first step is to trace the will of the male decedent's father-in-law. This could be accomplished by locating the will of the decedent's wife and working backward as before. However, a preliminary analysis should attempt to establish (1) the extent to which the sons of wealthy men marry the daughters of wealthy men, and (2) the role this plays in perpetuating the inequality of material wealth.

Further regression analysis of the father-son relationship should be carried out, going beyond the approach in chapter 4. This surely would take account of the time elapsed between a father's death and a son's death.[3] For example, the father's estate, appreciated at the going rate of return up to the 1956–57 period, would undoubtedly offer a better sta-tistical explanation of the son's wealth than the original estate.[4] Obviously even this elaborated father-son analysis would still leave many important factors out of the picture. It would be promising to analyze the actual amounts inherited individually by each decedent son and the dates of the inheritance. This information is presumably available on the probate records of the identified fathers.

The Wedgwood-Harbury decision to begin with a given sample of wealthy sons and work back to the wealth of their fathers also raises methodological questions.[5] In the first place, it would be desirable to go back further if possible. More important, an obvious and hopeful alterna-tive to this entire approach is to reverse the order of attack, an approach that is being attempted by Paul Menchik at the Institute for Research on

3. The age of the son at death would also be required as a variable in the regres-sion to take account of accumulation independent of inheritance proper. There are also reasons to recommend a logarithmic transformation of the original wealth variable.

4. Using the father's wealth as an explanatory variable raises important methodo-logical questions, since the starting point was a sample of wealthy sons. On the other hand, "explaining" the father's wealth by the son's wealth is questionable to say the least.

5. See Josiah Wedgwood, *The Economics of Inheritance* (Routledge, 1929, and Penguin, 1939); and C. D. Harbury, "Inheritance and the Distribution of Personal Wealth in Britain," *Economic Journal,* vol. 72 (December 1962), pp. 845–68.

Poverty at the University of Wisconsin.[6] It might be more efficient and potentially illuminating to start with a group of decedents about sixty years ago.[7] Their wealth and bequests to children (including bequests via the spouse) should be used to explain statistically the ultimate estates of the children. Another major advantage of starting with parents' wills is that this could lead to data on all siblings, rather than on one son alone. In addition to the father-son type of analysis, a standard technique from the analysis of variance could be invoked to partition the variance of wealth of the children into the sum of two components—the variation *within* sibling groups and the variation between sibling groups.[8] It would then be possible to devise a measure of the role of intergenerational transference in the overall inequality of wealth.[9]

Feasibility of a U.S. Study

No intergenerational analysis of the Harbury-Wedgwood type has been attempted in the United States until recently when Paul Menchik of the University of Wisconsin began his study. On the basis of an unpublished pilot study by Harbury in 1962–63 of 40–50 decedents in San Diego County, California, the prospects are encouraging. Despite the high proportion of "immigrants" in the sample (the father of only one of them had died in the same county), he traced over half the fathers—mainly by correspondence with relatives. A much better success ratio could be scored in a large, less transient metropolitan area and with more extended efforts to trace the fathers. Harbury also found county court officials generally very cooperative in searching files and providing photocopies of wills. All in all, producing this type of data seems entirely feasible, though

6. Preliminary results of his study were described in chapter 4.
7. Whether female decedents and heirs should be included in the analysis is not obvious. Certainly their inclusion would add to data-collecting problems.
8. More precisely the components are, respectively, (1) the weighted mean of group variances, and (2) the variance of weighted group means.
9. Polar cases would seem to be (1) complete and rigid intergenerational transmission of wealth—no variation of wealth within sibling groups; and (2) no intergenerational association—variation within sibling groups the same as overall variation. The logarithmic transformation of the wealth variable might improve prospects for this analysis by moving the distribution toward normality, or at least symmetry, and by facilitating measurement of the effects on inequality of special changes. (The transformation focuses attention on the *relative* distribution of wealth, since the variance of the logarithms of wealth is unaffected by a given percentage change for all holders.)

more difficult and expensive than in Britain where all records are in one place.

The best way to begin a U.S. data search of this type would be with a pilot study of a large central repository of probate records, such as in Cook County, Illinois. A sample of 500 to 1,000 recent male decedents, with the sampling rate varying positively with the wealth level, could be readily drawn.[10] Letters to persons mentioned in the son's will seems the logical first step in tracing fathers. If 80 percent of the information could be obtained that way at a trivial cost, as Harbury found in Britain, a substantial sample of recent decedents could be analyzed feasibly; the second step would be to check *Who's Who* and similar publications, and the residual follow-up efforts for 10 percent or so would not be overly taxing. The only special difficulty confronting a U.S. analysis of the intergenerational relationship of wills is the decentralized location of records. But Harbury's success through correspondence with local authorities suggests that this approach is promising. If it should prove inefficient, consideration could be given to the meaning of a sample of sons restricted to those whose fathers' last residence was in Cook County.

The alternative approach could start with a sample of fathers who, for example, died in Cook County about 60 years ago. Then an attempt could be made to trace the wills of their children. In any case a pilot study of one location appears in order, whether the initial sample is to be taken of the first or second generation, or both. Such a pilot study would make possible an assessment of the feasibility of a nationwide study, but it is very likely to be deserving of analysis in its own right. As an alternative to an analysis of wills, an attempt could be made to match father and son estate tax returns in Wisconsin, where the returns are available for research purposes.

The Separation of Pre-Inheritance Influences on Wealth from the Effects of Bequests

With some official cooperation, a promising effort could be made to separate different types of intergenerational influences. Beginning in 1966, federal estate tax returns added a section in which the executor is directed

10. Obviously some thought needs to be given to the appropriate wealth range for study. There is no need to restrict the analysis to very high brackets, as Harbury did. Tracing father-son links, however, is probably more difficult the lower the wealth level. Furthermore, tracing the wills of mothers and parents-in-law should also be considered.

to furnish the name, social security number, and bequests assigned to each heir. It has been suggested that for a sample of the estate tax returns already available to researchers, the Treasury could match each return with the income tax returns to beneficiaries. Such a project has been under consideration at the Treasury for some time. Alternatively, information on heirs could be obtained from the wills that are required to be filed with estate tax returns. Then it would be possible to match each estate tax return with the heir's income tax return information in the master file.[11]

If this exercise were undertaken, the resulting data would offer a major alternative to the previously described analysis of probated wills. It would provide a basis for further analysis of intergenerational wealth relationships along the lines just discussed, with the income or estimated wealth of the children being the dependent variable in this case. The data for sibling heirs would be especially valuable for the reasons already mentioned. The wealth of the living would be related to that of their parents without waiting for the prospective heirs to die. The association could first be analyzed before and then after imputing the proceeds of the estate going to the heirs.

The relationship existing before the ultimate material inheritance would cast new light on the intergenerational transmission of wealth. It would suggest the extent to which environmental advantage is created by familial position even before the impact of the actual bequests. The wealth of the decedent could be interpreted as a proxy for the advantages offered to prospective heirs by favorable environment, educational opportunity, gifts, and the like made possible by family wealth. This is not to imply that parental wealth alone can explain all of the advantages of one child over another. Obviously they vary in native ability to accumulate wealth; and nonwealthy parents may promote education and other aids to material success. The point here is simply that these Treasury data would make possible an analysis of just what part of the wealth of a child can be explained by the wealth of the parent, independently of any ultimate inheritance. Other explanatory variables such as age would, of course, be needed in any model explaining children's wealth.[12]

11. To find the tax return itself is apparently not feasible in most cases, but adequate information appears to be available in the master file.
12. An objection to this, as well as to the studies proposed earlier, may be that parental wealth per se may not be the real cause of the better life changes of the child. The expected intergenerational association of wealth could reflect in part a tendency for children of the wealthy to inherit an ability to accumulate. This qualification needs more consideration, since the policy called for, if any, would presum-

This type of analysis of children's wealth before inheritance could have significant policy implications. If the wealth of a parent during his lifetime has a strong positive effect on the wealth of his children, this offers one reason why estate and inheritance taxes may be relatively slow and feeble devices for reducing inequality. Furthermore, a knowledge of the bequests to each child (in addition to the taxable wealth of the deceased) offers evidence on the contrasting impact of estate taxes and inheritance taxes. If there is substantial variation in the size of the bequests to siblings, an equity case can be made for taxing the share of each beneficiary in relation to *his* inheritance, rather than by a single tax on the estate.[13]

Perhaps an even more important contribution that could be made by a match-up of estate tax returns with heirs' income tax returns is to reveal the importance of inheritance proper and the effect of the tax on the estate. It would be possible to show for each heir just what the inheritance did to change his wealth position at the time of its receipt. (See discussion in chapter 1 of J. Paul Getty.) A knowledge of the immediate effect of inheritance on heirs' wealth would be extremely valuable. If data from the decedent's last full-year income tax return were also tracked down by the Treasury in the master file, the incomes of the two generations could be related as well. Moreover, the availability of data for siblings would make possible the kind of analysis of variance previously suggested.

Theoretical Analysis of the Life Cycle: The Accumulation, Transfer, and Taxation Process

As mentioned in chapters 1 and 3, several dynamic models have been developed recently that portray individual accumulation, bequest, and tax-paying behavior. In the simplest form developed by Modigliani and Brumberg, the net worth profile depends on the rate of return and saving.[14] No bequests emerge, since dissaving is assumed to exhaust lifetime accumulation. This type of model has been extended to allow for population growth, the bequest motive for saving, and tax effects, as in the

---

ably be different from that called for by simple material and environmental advantage.

13. Still more equitable would be a tax based on the prior wealth of each heir.

14. Franco Modigliani and Richard Brumberg, "Utility Analysis and the Consumption Function: An Interpretation of Cross-Section Data," in Kenneth K. Kurihara, ed., *Post Keynesian Economics* (Rutgers University Press, 1954).

work of A. B. Atkinson.[15] A further elaboration by Alan Blinder builds in the marital selection process and various forms of estate division.[16] Despite their very abstract structures, these models have important implications for the real world. Further theoretical work is clearly called for, especially on the role of transfers in maintaining inequality and on the potential of taxation. It is even conceivable that the models could eventually be vested with empirical content.

Simulation Studies

A promising approach is the microsimulation model in the tradition of Orcutt and others.[17] Empirically grounded microsimulations have been under way for some time at the Urban Institute. Only recently has this work been oriented explicitly to the problem of intergenerational wealth transmission. Completely a priori microsimulations by Frederic Pryor and Alan Blinder focus directly on such intergenerational relationships as marital selection, fertility rates, and inheritance, as well as on government intervention in the distribution of wealth and income.[18] These are very interesting simulation studies, but so far they are without empirical content. It should be noted that the elaborate simulations by Pryor and Blinder led them to opposing conclusions on the importance of the marital selection pattern for the maintenance of inequality. This suggests that these simulation models of wealth distribution would be much more promising if they could be built into an empirically grounded study.

The simulation model of a sample of households could be launched under the actual "initial conditions" of some period earlier in the twentieth century. For example, it could start with Lampman's 1922 wealth distribution and the income distribution of that time and move the house-

15. A. B. Atkinson, "A Model of the Distribution of Wealth," working paper (Massachusetts Institute of Technology, 1974; processed).

16. Alan S. Blinder, "A Model of Inherited Wealth," *Quarterly Journal of Economics*, vol. 87 (November 1973), pp. 608–26.

17. See Guy H. Orcutt and others, *Microanalysis of Socioeconomic Systems: A Simulation Study* (Harper, 1961).

18. Frederic L. Pryor, "Simulation of the Impact of Social and Economic Institutions on the Size Distribution of Income and Wealth," *American Economic Review*, vol. 63 (March 1973), pp. 50–72; and Blinder, "A Model of Inherited Wealth." For comments on the work of Pryor and Blinder, see Atkinson and Harrison, *The Distribution of Personal Wealth in Britain*, chap. 8.

holds forward through time.[19] The model would impose patterns of marriage, birth, divorce, empirically grounded tax functions, and various behavioral relations. The wealth transmission process could be studied within this framework. The correlation of the economic status of marital partners would be built into the model. Random numbers generated within the computer would decree the death of a wealthholder in a given year according to the probability associated with his age, sex, and race. His wealth would be distributed to heirs according to some probability distribution based on empirical studies. Human wealth would be inherited according to the relationships and probabilities analyzed in the literature on human capital. Attempts should be made by successive approximations to generate wealth and income distributions actually observed in recent years. Given a functioning model, it would then be possible to simulate the effect of changes in marital selection patterns, gift and bequest habits, taxes and subsidies. The objective would be to assess the extent to which changes in behavior and policies would mold the wealth distribution toward equality, how fast, and how far.

Wisconsin Evidence on the Effectiveness of the Transmission of Wealth to Heirs

As the basis for their longitudinal study of individual incomes in Wisconsin, David and Miller traced a sample of thousands of taxpayers over a period of 12 years.[20] During this period many disappeared from the income tax roster, of whom about 500 are believed to have died. This is a rich body of available data for appraisal of the extent to which income recipients succeed in peeling off portions of their wealth so that it does not appear later in their estates.

Since Wisconsin tax returns are available for research purposes, it should be feasible to trace the inheritance tax returns of the deceased for comparison with their income histories. The year-by-year wealth of each individual could be estimated by capitalizing the investment income on his tax return. The level and trends of lifetime wealth estimates could

19. See Robert J. Lampman, *The Share of Top Wealth-Holders in the National Wealth, 1922–56* (Princeton University Press for the National Bureau of Economic Research, 1962).

20. Martin David and Roger Miller, "A Naive History of Individual Incomes in Wisconsin, 1947–1959," *Review of Income and Wealth,* Series 16 (March 1970), pp. 79–116.

then be analyzed for comparison with inheritance data. A tendency for the wealth of individuals to decline in the years before death, or even to rise less than aggregate wealth per capita, would be evidence of a splitting up of wealth during the taxpayer's lifetime.

The second part of this analysis of Wisconsin data would entail tracing at least the latest of the income tax returns of the specified heirs. Again the investment income could be capitalized into wealth estimates for correlation with the wealth of the decedents. The four-step link from the income of the decedent to his wealth to the bequests to each heir to the income of each heir should offer new insights on intergenerational relationships.

Case Studies of the Effect of Gifts, Bequests, and Wealth Taxes on Recipients

An alternative to the approaches discussed earlier is a direct analysis of the role of gifts and inheritance in the wealth of the living. Many lists of top wealthholders have been compiled in the past, but the *Fortune* studies by Smith and Louis reported in 1957, 1968, and 1973 offer the most current picture.[21] These studies deal explicitly but only in very broad terms with the role of inheritance in the building of fortunes. The 1968 study asserts that inheritance has been declining as a source of great wealth and that federal estate and gift taxes "have been decimating the great old fortunes." But the 1957 study quotes the president of a large trust company as saying that "Uncle Sam isn't taking the big estates." These are strong, important, and contradictory assertions for which little evidence is presented. These studies generated a massive amount of data based on hundreds of interviews with surprisingly cooperative respondents. The great bulk of the information is unpublished; if it could be further analyzed and supplemented by public records, it could make a major contribution to unraveling the effects of inheritance, of other forms of accumulation, and of taxation. Isolating the importance of inheritance would not be easy, but data on its original size, date of receipt, and the current

21. Richard Austin Smith, "The Fifty-Million-Dollar Man," *Fortune,* November 1957, pp. 176 ff.; Arthur M. Louis, "America's Centimillionaires," ibid., May 1968, pp. 152 ff.; and Arthur M. Louis, "The New Rich of the Seventies," ibid., September 1973, pp. 170 ff.

aggregate wealth of the individual would provide the basis for a promising analysis.[22]

A second direct approach to analysis of the role of material inheritance in the current wealth distribution is that offered by surveys. Two potentially useful surveys are already available:

1. Robin Barlow, Harvey E. Brazer, and James N. Morgan, *Economic Behavior of the Affluent* (Brookings Institution, 1966). High-income respondents were asked what fraction of their total assets was accounted for by gifts and inheritance, respectively.

2. Dorothy S. Projector and Gertrude S. Weiss, *Survey of Financial Characteristics of Consumers* (Board of Governors of the Federal Reserve System, 1966). This survey contained less explicit inheritance questions than those of Barlow, Brazer, and Morgan (and did not cover gifts at all). Each respondent was asked in effect whether the family's inherited assets as a fraction of total assets was "none," "small," or "substantial." Further evaluation of the role of inheritance on the basis of these surveys might be fruitful.

General Regression Models of Wealth Determination

Another means of evaluating the importance of intergenerational influences is cross-sectional regression analysis. Models should be designed to explain the material wealth of the living by means of specified intergenerational factors and other variables. Projector and Weiss have already attempted in their study to explain wealth by income, age, employment status, and inheritance received. Further regression analysis with the available tapes is in order for several reasons. Much more experimentation with structural forms of the explanatory models is called

22. For example, suppose A and B are both worth $1 million today and that this represents an appreciation of 10 percent and 12 percent respectively on their known inheritances 20 years ago. Assume further that the going rate of return based on security market indexes had been 10 percent in that period. Thus A scored no net gain attributable to prior wealth or above-average later rates of return. His situation is just what it would be if he had achieved the standard rate of capital growth on an original inheritance of about $145,000. In this sense all his wealth is attributable to the original inheritance. However, B's 12 percent yield implies that he received only a $100,000 inheritance. Thus only 100/145, or 69 percent, of B's wealth can be attributed to his inheritance and the rest to preexisting wealth or to his achievement of a relatively high rate of return.

for. Responses to the inheritance question have not been utilized as efficiently as possible. Finally, the available inventory of variables has not been adequately utilized. Valuable information on income source, family size, and education of head was available but was not tapped in the analysis.

Age, Sex, and Race Factors in Wealth Inequality

The previously discussed regression analysis by Projector and Weiss of individual households should be supplemented by an explicit study of age, sex, and race factors. Although not usually thought of as inherited characteristics, age, sex, and race are clearly "received" by the individual and (like inherited material wealth) are deserving of analytical separation from other determinants of wealth over which the individual has at least some control. Wealth differentials associated with saving over the age cycle would persist even under a situation of complete equality among those of a given age. This raises the question of the relative importance of this benign form of inequality in the overall distribution. The significance of age and sex differences can be studied effectively via the estate tax distributions. More work should be done comparing the degree of inequality within age classes to overall inequality, as discussed in chapter 3. Preliminary evidence reported in that chapter showed little difference, thereby deflating the argument that much of inequality is due simply to a natural lifetime saving pattern. The same analysis should be applied more extensively to the U.S. data with respect to both age and sex. A more general quantitative approach for both types of classification would be an analysis of variance. In the case of age the ratio of the variance within age classes to total variance would be a measure of the fraction of total variance not attributable to age differentials.[23] The evidence in chapter 3 suggests that this ratio will be near zero. This would be an important finding, if backed by detailed evidence.

Statistical information on wealth differentials by race is less adequate for age and sex. A similar analysis is in order, however. Two studies based on the 1967 Survey of Economic Opportunity data were done a few years

23. The logarithmic transformation of the wealth variable would be appropriate in such an analysis.

ago by Terrell and by Birnbaum and Weston.[24] The latter have explored an apparent contradiction in the survey data. In the first place, the evidence disputes Banfield's "present minded" thesis by indicating high black saving rates relative to income.[25] But the figures also indicate relatively low net worth at a given income level, which Birnbaum and Weston attribute to inferior investment opportunity for blacks. A promising research project dealing with wealth differentials by race was completed in 1971 by James D. Smith.[26] He was able to link up District of Columbia inheritance tax returns with vital statistics records containing many data, including race. It would be useful to revitalize this study and carry out an analysis of variance to measure the role of race in overall wealth inequality in the District of Columbia.

24. See Henry S. Terrell, "Wealth Accumulation of Black and White Families: The Empirical Evidence," *Journal Of Finance,* vol. 26 (May 1971), pp. 363–77; and Howard Birnbaum and Rafael Weston, "Homeownership and the Wealth Position of Black and White Americans," *Review of Income and Wealth,* vol. 20 (March 1974), pp. 103–18. The Survey of Economic Opportunity was conducted by the U.S. Bureau of the Census for the U.S. Office of Economic Opportunity.

25. Edward C. Banfield, *The Unheavenly City* (Little, Brown, 1970).

26. James D. Smith, "White Wealth and Black People: The Distribution of Wealth in Washington, D.C., in 1967," in Smith, ed., *The Personal Distribution of Income and Wealth* (Columbia University Press for the National Bureau of Economic Research, 1975), chap. 11.

Index

Aitchison, J., 83n
Allen, R. G. D., 26n, 36n
Atkinson, A. B., 4–6n, 8n, 11, 20, 51n, 52, 53, 55n, 56, 57n, 58, 59, 61n, 66–68, 89n, 95

Banfield, Edward C., 100
Barlow, Robin, 16n, 98
Birnbaum, Howard, 100
Blinder, Alan S., 20, 86, 95
Bossons, John, 17n
Brazer, Harvey E., 16n, 98
Brittain, John A., 10n, 15n, 49n, 82n, 88n
Brumberg, Richard, 52n, 54n, 94

Cates, Judith N., 42n, 87n
Consumer financial characteristics, 18
Cooper, George, 4n

David, Martin, 96

Economic inequality, 1, 2
Economic status, 1n, 2, 73
Estates: father's, 75–78, 80, 81, 82n, 92; involving community property, 28; taxes, 4, 5, 22n, 28, 37n, 82, 88, 93, 94, 97, 99; trusts, 5–6

Father-son wealth relationships. See Estates; Inheritance; Wealth
Federal Reserve survey, 69
Feldstein, Martin, 5, 6, 53n, 71
Franklin, Stephen D., 4n, 20n, 68n, 86

Galton, Francis, 85
Getty, J. Paul, 15, 16, 30n, 49
Goldsmith, Raymond W., 17n

Hansen, W. Lee, 7, 8n
Harbury, D. D., 27, 30, 31n, 75–87, 89, 91, 92
Harrison, A. J., 4n, 5n, 61n, 89, 95n
Harriss, C. Lowell, 5n

Hitchens, D. M. W. N., 27, 30, 31n, 77n, 78, 80, 81

Income: annuity, 8n; inequality, 7, 8; economic, 7
Inheritance: analyses, 42–46; determinants models, 42–43; father-son relationship, 77–79, 87; individual, 10, 23n; intergenerational, 9, 14, 17, 21–23, 28, 50, 56, 73–75, 77, 88, 89, 93; and life-cycle relationship, 53, 77; male-female accrual, 42; and marital selection, 10, 90; sons and daughters, 44, 45, 90; and wealth inequality, 51, 97; wealth ratios, 48, 49
Inman, Walter P., Jr., 15
Intergenerational transfers: as basis of women's wealth, 21, 25–27, 31, 42, 47, 50; of economic status, 73; effect on wealth accumulation, 59, 76, 80, 86, 90, 91n, 93, 95–97; inheritance, 9, 14, 17, 21–23, 28, 50, 56, 73–75, 77, 88, 89, 93; material, 17, 73, 74, 98; and personal wealth, 51; ratio for married persons, 24, 32, 42, 46, 47; ratio to total wealth, 23, 47, 48, 86
Internal Revenue Service (IRS), 3n, 5n, 19, 24, 32, 33
Investments. See Wealth accumulation

Jantscher, Gerald R., 4n, 60n

Knight, Frank H., 1n
Kurihara, Kenneth K., 52n, 94n

Lampman, Robert J., 4, 5n, 17, 18n, 19, 26, 95, 96
Lansing, John B., 86, 87n
Lebergott, Stanley, 3n, 19, 20n
Life-cycle hypothesis, 51–53, 55, 59, 62, 65, 67, 76, 79, 94; earnings relationship, 58, 66; model, 94, 95; Modigliani-Brumberg model, 54, 94; Oulton model, 58; quasi-empirical